Dick Hrebik—first, foremost, and forever a Marine, and award-winning author of *So, You Want a Job?*, *Corps Vet*, and *The Warrior Among Us*—has written yet another enthralling book. In this World War II biography, Hrebik takes us inside the mind of the late Captain Walter H. Beckham Jr., USNR, Ret., as he personally recounts the first time he felt the war up close and personal during an attack upon his ship by Japanese fighter planes off Midway Island, to his long years after World War II as the practicing attorney he had planned to become before the Japanese attack on Pearl Harbor changed all that. *Walter Goes to War—WWII* is a very worthwhile read about another of our Greatest Generation who have left us all too soon. I highly recommend this book!

~Marc Yablonka
Author of *Distant War: Recollections of Vietnam, Laos and Cambodia* (Navigator Books)

Guys like Walter are leaving us in droves these days and so many of their stories will never be told—BRAVO to DICK HREBIK for chronicling this mainly WWII biography. The description of Japan's long journey from being an insular medieval society to becoming a modern world power to be reckoned with was well done. The author managed to distill a very complicated history of over a hundred years into less than twenty-five well-written pages of salient facts. Japan was a world military power at the beginning of WWII and even though having lost, is still a world economic power.

The description of Walter's participation in battles starting with Midway was extremely vivid. The reader could well imagine being there. Walter's notoriety as a pioneer legal legend makes this book a MUST READ!

~Walter D. Banks
Commander—USNR Ret. Naval Aviator

WALTER GOES TO WAR—WWII

A BIOGRAPHY OF

CAPTAIN WALTER H. BECKHAM JR., USNR RETIRED

WALTER GOES TO WAR—WWII

Windy City Publishers
2118 Plum Grove Rd., #349
Rolling Meadows, IL 60008
www.windycitypublishers.com

Published in the United States of America

First Edition: 2013

ISBN:
978-1-935766-85-8

Library of Congress Control Number:
2013949306

WALTER GOES TO WAR—WWII

A BIOGRAPHY OF

CAPTAIN WALTER H. BECKHAM JR., USNR RETIRED

BY DICK HREBIK

Appreciation

Oftentimes the reader may recognize why this story is very personal to me because many of the following people were or are friends of mine, to whom I owe an additional debt of gratitude: Walter, his wife, Ethel, their three children, Barbara DeLeo, Walter Beckham III, and James Beckham, and grandson, Justin Beckham, for sharing their memories and letters; my wife, Carole Hrebik, who dug out Walter's memoirs titled Naval Engagements; my cousin, Army Air Corps Captain Joe Roubal, who was an older brother to me; Vice Admiral Bill Martin, for befriending me and taking me to some memorable football games at the Naval Academy; Lorraine Rogers, who became as accomplished an artist as she was an Army Air Corps pilot in WWII; retired Marine Colonel Warren Weidhahn for information on the Azorian story; Susan Cruse and Tom Brodnax of Emory University, for researching and providing pictures and information related to Walter's Emory Medalist recognition; my former neighbors of Company B, 192nd Tank Battalion, who experienced the Bataan Death March; and CVS drugstore manager Heather O'Bday, who helped me with the picture of the USS *Portland*; and the entire Windy City Publishers team, especially the sage editor, Janet Dooley, and supurb freelance editor, Carol Kiley.

When writing of historical events, many days are spent researching, which cannot be done without the assistance of others. The following people deserve special recognition for helping me in this endeavor: Navy Captain Henry J. Hendrix, II and the National Museum of the US Navy for assistance in getting two documents declassified for inclusion in this book; the Ships Data Section of the Navy Department's Office of Public Relations for providing the history of the USS *Portland;* the POW Research Network Japan for information regarding the B-29 bombings of Japan; Archive Specialist Susan Nash, Archive Technicians David Szucs and Del May of the National Personnel Records Center for providing a copy of Captain Beckham's personnel file; Denise Mathis, Administrative Assistant to the Mount Olive Schools system, for researching Joe Roubal's high school records; Maria S. Johnson's Jul/Aug 2009, article in *The Florida Bar Journal* regarding the restoration of the historic Courtroom 6-1 in the Dade County Courthouse, Miami, FL; courtroom bailiff, Mark Guzman, a fellow Marine reconner, for showing me the famous courtroom; Eunice Sigler, Public Relations Director for 11th Judicial Circuit of Florida for digging through the archives and providing the dimensions of the famous Courtroom 6-1; and the numerous Internet sites, including Wikipedia, which again saved me a lot of research time.

Dick's Maxims

Look to the past to better see the future.

Know the difference between doing things right
and doing the right thing.

The young do not yet know what they don't know.

Nobody ever drowned in sweat.

Life is not infinite—use it wisely.

There is little in life worth falling on your sword over.

There is a whole world out there—
reach out and take a bite—
don't live in a hole.

Contents

CHAPTER 1

WAR ON THE HORIZON

"Force, no matter how concealed, begets resistance."
Lakota Indian saying

Walter Hull Beckham Jr. planned to become a lawyer, as was his father before him. Judge Walter H. Beckham Sr. served on the Florida Dade County Juvenile and Domestic Relations Court from 1932 until 1960. In 1960, he became the first American judge to serve as president of the International Congress of Juvenile Court Judges. Those were big shoes to fill by all accounts, but the quiet, mild-mannered Walter Jr. was up to the task.

Unfortunately, the world had something else in mind. Walter Jr. would face a different challenge, one that would lead him into a violent, deadly environment on the eve of starting his legal career, and one that he accepted without hesitation, immediately setting out his plan as to how he would participate. Years later, he advised his son, Walter III, to "Always have a plan for everything in life. Don't run pell-mell into anything without a plan." That was how Walter Hull Beckham Jr. led his life. Even while still in high school, the learned scholar Beckham felt and smelled the winds of war blowing through the royal palm trees of Miami, across the oceans from Asia and Europe. And Walter had a plan.

JAPAN

The forces that were about to so violently impact Walter's life had begun nearly a century earlier. In 1854, Japanese Shoguns started sending representatives to Western countries, including the United States, to learn Western arts and sciences. They wanted to compete with Western powers, rather than be dominated by them. A secondary, and far more evil reason, was to learn how the Japanese might dominate the rest of the world. This was evidenced in the late 1800s when Japan decided it had learned all it needed to know about its future enemies to defeat them. The Shoguns started promoting Hakko Ichiu, which loosely translates to a plan to rule all the eight corners of the world under one roof. After all, China had ruled the Far East for thousands of years. Now it was time for China's little neighbor to take it down and control the new Far East, if not the entire globe. Whereas Western minds approach national and international change through the strategic actions they plan to take in the coming decade, Orientals envision change without regard to how long it will take, and only focus on the road to achieve the goal—maybe not in one life, but in a second life if need be.

The year 1868 saw Japanese Emperor Meiji end the feudal system, putting the Samurai warlords out of business, as he modernized Japan through his Meiji Restoration program. He knew Japan needed to become industrialized in order to compete in the international market. One of the first steps in that direction was the Ganghwa Treaty of 1876 between the Empire of Japan and the Kingdom of Joseon (Korea), which opened Korean ports to Japanese trade. During this same period of time, other countries became interested in Asia. The Sino-French War of 1884-85 saw France win control of Vietnam. The 1885 Convention of Tientsin forged an agreement between China and Japan for each to withdraw its troops from Korea, allowing Korea to become a sovereign state. But neither abided by the agreement and both countries continued to control this tiny nation that wanted to break free and take its own seat on the world stage.

When it came to naval matters and how to control the oceans, Japan looked to Great Britain as a model for its navy. The British Royal Navy was considered the best in the world at that time, and British advisors taught Japanese sailors the arts of seamanship and gunnery. As a result, many Japanese ships were built in English and French shipyards. As for its army, instead of exchanging military doctrine with France, it chose the Prussian Army model, thereby establishing a close relationship with Germany. This new relationship went unnoticed by other countries for decades. And by 1890, Japan had a modern, professionally trained Western-style army and navy of substantial size. No other country seemed to be concerned as to why Japan was preparing a war machine right under their noses.

The stage was set. Corruption in China saw money for battleships go to building the magnificent Summer Palace in Beijing. The Qing Dynasty didn't even have a national army. Their military was split into regional armies of Manchu, Mongol, Hui (Muslim), and Han armies, all of which ignored pleas for help from the Beijing army and navy when, in 1894, Japan invaded China. Japan called it the "holy war" against the Qing Dynasty, better known as the first Sino-Japanese War. The first battle was the invasion of Seoul, when Japan captured the Korean emperor, supplanting him with its own pro-Japanese government. The new government effectively terminated all previous agreements with China and ordered all Chinese troops to leave Korea. This model is used yet today; when one nation invades another, it removes and replaces the existing ruler with the head of an opposition party thought to be loyal and friendly to the invading country.

Why the United States and other countries thought China would crush any Japanese invasion is not known. Was poor intelligence the origin of this mistake? To this day, no one has come forward with an answer to this question. When German General Staff Officer William Lang, advisor to the Chinese military at the time, was interviewed by Reuters, he stated he and many other nations believed Japan would lose. Might he have misled the world to protect Germany's secret allegiance to Japan? Do the answers lie buried in someone's intelligence archives? Possibly a future historian will uncover these unknowns. The fact is, the war was of short duration, ending in 1895. Approximately 35,000 Chinese and 12,000 Japanese died in the war. In early 1895, Japan attacked and took the Pescadores Islands, cutting off Chinese resupply to Taiwan. The Japanese Imperial Army soundly defeated the Chinese Army in a small but decisive war, thus requiring China to cede Taiwan to Japan, and giving Korea its independence under the Treaty of Shimonoseki. Japan needed the vast rice fields of Korea to feed its growing army, and Korean coal and iron ore to build its industrial and military complexes. It was time for Japan to now regroup and prepare for the next phase of their Hakko Ichiu.

Looking back, the Chinese Empire had been in various stages of turmoil for a long time. Beginning with the Opium War of 1839-1842, several European powers had exacted deals with China to control portions of the empire, including Germany, which had seized Kiaochow and Tsingtao in 1897. Anti-foreign sentiments broiled over when the I Ho Ch'uan (Righteous Harmonious Fists), better known as the Boxers, rebelled against foreigners in an attempt to rid their country of all people except Chinese. Sporadic fighting continued in many quarters as allied troops from Great Britain, Germany, Russia, France, the United States, Italy, Austria, and Japan fought to rescue their legations and diplomatic corps from the marauding Boxers. Not until February 1, 1901, did the Chinese authorities agree to abolish the Boxer Society, ending the rebellion. On September 7, 1901, the Peace Protocol of Peking returned diplomatic relations with China's allied nations to normal. But the Qing Dynasty was so weakened it was overthrown by the Republic of China in 1912.

All of this meant opportunity for Japan. In Japan's mind, China had been neutered and could no longer protect itself from foreign invasion. Japan began to put its pieces into place. The 1904-05 Russo-Japanese War resulted in the Portsmouth Treaty, wherein Russia proclaimed Japan had the primary political, military, and economic interests in Korea over all other nations. It also kept Russia out of Manchuria and Korea.

In the Eulsa Treaty of 1905, Japan denied Korea its right to sovereignty. Instead, it made Korea a protectorate of Japan, officially annexing it in 1910. It wasn't until 1965 that Japan and South Korea jointly declared both the 1905 and 1910 "agreements" null and void.

In 1910, on the other side of the globe, the Mexican Revolution erupted as a result of a fixed election. At that time, Mexico was deeply involved financially and economically with Imperial Germany, a relationship complicated by the growing influence of the United States. With several of the Mexican states mounting a civil war for control of all of Mexico, Germany saw an opportunity to leverage its support of the Mexican government against the United States. Germany aligned with Japan in 1914, saying it would offer assistance to Mexico if Japan agreed to invade the United States. Germany believed the United States would get involved in the Mexican Revolution, thereby stretching its military forces in two different directions. Germany calculated the United States could not then help Great Britain and France defend against invasion by Germany. But the United States sent troops to Vera Cruz to form a blockade, preventing German weapons and munitions from landing and supporting Mexico. Soon thereafter, an agreement was reached with Mexico that the United States would withdraw its troops if Mexico would not attack the United States.

There is a wonderful story about this time, actually a year earlier, when the Mexican revolutionary Pancho Villa was about to attack the city of Juarez, Mexico, in October. Speaking with an American journalist friend, Norman Walker, Pancho Villa is said to have told his pistoleros "We shall hold off the attack until the Americans finish their ball game," referring to the major league baseball World Series between the New York Giants and Philadelphia Athletics, which the Athletics won four games to one. A few years later, when the United States supported the Mexican government instead of Pancho Villa, he did invade. When General "Black Jack" Pershing was sent to chase Pancho Villa and his pistoleros back into Mexico, he did. But he never caught Pancho Villa himself.

In 1915, Japan further flexed its muscle by issuing the "Twenty-One Demands," which took certain political and commercial privileges from China. One might think of it as the first embargo on a nation in modern times.

All the signs were present, but few paid any attention to the growing "winds of war" blowing from this tiny nation. Japan was systematically weakening China in preparation for an all-out invasion of the entire Chinese mainland, at a time of Japan's own choosing. Japan continued to foment civil unrest among the Chinese people against their own government, fueled by the Kuomintang (KMT) National Revolutionary Army (NRA) attacks on several regional warlords. The Mukden Incident was one such event. Japanese soldiers placed a small amount of dynamite on a railroad track they controlled in the eastern region of China near the Manchurian border, with the intent of blowing up a train. Though the dynamite was insufficient to damage trains passing over the tracks hours later, Japan claimed Chinese dissidents had placed it there, giving cause to launch a full invasion of Manchuria in September of 1931. Japan no longer needed to comfortably sit, watch, and applaud the revolt from within. Everything was going its way, and Emperor Hirohito was pleased.

The Manchurian invasion accomplished the first two goals for invading all of China. Japan gained access to the raw materials of the region to support a market for its manufactured goods, and two, it created a buffer zone between Japan and the Soviet Union, which Japan was not yet ready to tackle. It was a well thought out, realistic plan to take one country at a time, using the materials and manpower of each conquered nation to attack its neighbor. This was how great conquerors such as Alexander the Great and Genghis Khan strategized so successfully long ago. Japan was in control of its own destiny, and the other larger super powers were oceans away. Surely they would not care or be interested in interfering. Years passed, but finally Western allies did interfere with Japan's master plan.

In 1933, when Walter Beckham was in junior high, Japan attacked the Rehe province, or Great Wall region, creating another buffer zone between the Wall and Peiping-Tianjin. China was on its heels and requested protection from the League of Nations. The League, unwilling to engage in a military confrontation, did nothing to stop Japan beyond condemning its actions in the press. With each step, Japan became more emboldened with a growing belief it was invincible. Japan felt it could truly rule the world and no other nation or nations could stop it. Unknown to many at the time, Japan had, in fact, entered into a secret pact with Germany to advance on two separate continents, eventually attacking the United States as its final battle.

INVASION OF CHINA

Calling it the Specialization of North China, or the North China Autonomous Movement, Japan established local governments loyal to itself in five Chinese provinces. Now Japan had created a foothold in China without significant military action. Seizing an opportunity to divide and conquer, Japan pitted the KMT (strongest political party in China) against the reigning Chinese government. In 1935, the Japanese engineered the signing of the He-Umezu Agreement, which forbade the KMT from engaging in political party gatherings in either Mongolia or northern Hebei. Later that same year the KMT was even forced to leave the Chabar province. Today, the KMT is the ruling party in Taiwan. By year's end, Japan, through its puppet political councils, ruled all of Northern China. The year 1936 saw the installation of the Mongol Military Government, providing all the necessary military and economic aid Japan needed. Another giant step in the march across China had been taken and all the partisan forces were in place. The KMT had not the wherewithal to defend itself. *Bonzai! Bonzai!* was sounded at the Marco Polo Bridge to Beiping (Beijing) on July 7, 1937. The Imperial Japanese Army (IJA) quickly and easily defeated the Chinese Army infantry divisions located in its northwest region. Beiping and Tianjin were under Japanese control, and the world still stood by and watched.

Politics had already influenced how the "war" was to be prosecuted, and how it was perceived by other nations, specifically the United Kingdom and the United States. Internationally, the Japanese invasion of China was referred to as an "incident," because neither country had declared war on the other. How many times have politicians played with semantics when identifying whether fighting between nations is or is not war. This same mentality was used when the fighting in Korea was designated a conflict, not a war, by the U.S. Congress. For all the men who fought and died there, it was a war, no matter what Washington called it. Japan's primary source of steel and petroleum was the United States, and they wanted us to stay out of it. They knew full well the U.S. Congress had passed Neutrality Acts earlier in the decade. Following our involvement in WWI, the acts were intended to keep us out of the growing turmoil in Europe and Asia. Had "war" been declared by either side, President Roosevelt would have been obliged to impose an embargo on Japan in compliance with our Neutrality Acts. We acted like the German Guard Sergeant Schultz, a character in the television show *Hogan's Heroes*, who always said, "I see nothing, I know nothing."

"Enough is enough," or so Chinese Generalissimo Chiang Kai-shek might have said. Ignoring the agreements and edicts of Japan, he mobilized the central government's military and attacked the Japanese Marines in Shanghai on August 13, 1937. Japan didn't back down. It was going to hold onto China, no matter the cost. It immediately pumped 200,000 troops into Shanghai, and after three months of hard fighting, regained control of the region.

During the battle of Shanghai, the seeds of an idea, which would have a great impact on the future of the war, were formulated in the mind of a U.S. Marine. The Sixth Marine Regiment had been sent to help the Fourth Marine Regiment, which was already there to protect American interests and help evacuate Americans from China. Among these troops was an intelligence officer, Lieutenant (later Lieutenant General) Victor H. "Brute" Krulak. Later recognized as one of the most intelligent, courageous, military tacticians in the history of our country, he sought out a position from which he could observe the Japanese amphibious landing on the Yangtze River. Using a camera with a telephoto lens, he secretly photographed the action. The "Brute" witnessed the entire landing and took particular note of the landing craft used by the Japanese to unload their soldiers from their ships onto the land. He is quoted in the book *First Command*, written by Dwight Zimmerman, as follows, "There we saw, in action, exactly what the Marines had been looking for, a sturdy ramp-bow-type boat capable of transporting troops and heavy vehicles, depositing them directly on the beaches."

After submitting his report and photographs "up the chain," Washington bureaucracy being what it is, even in what was then the War Department, Krulak heard nothing for two years. When he inquired about his idea, Krulak found his report in a dead file labeled "the work of some nut out in China." But "Brute" persevered. He knew he had the answer. This boat was what the Marine Corps needed as it planned future amphibious landings against the Japanese in the Pacific, so Krulak took matters into his own hands. He built a balsa wood model of the Japanese landing crafts with retractable ramps, just as he had seen while stationed in China. He took his model to Andrew Higgins at the Higgins Industries boat building company in New Orleans. In three days Higgins had built a model. The Marine Corps was ecstatic, and the Higgins boat—officially named a Landing Craft Vehicle Personnel (LCVP)—became the single most valuable piece of equipment used in WWII. The islands of Iwo Jima, Guadalcanal, and Okinawa, as well as the beaches of Normandy, would never have been taken without the plywood constructed Higgins boat with its steel ramp. Supreme Allied Commander Dwight Eisenhower said "Andrew Higgins…is the man who won the war for us."

There is another far less important, but intriguing, story that also came out of Shanghai in 1937. For eight years archaeologists had been excavating hundreds of human fossils of a 680,000 to 780,000-year-old *Homo erectus*, known as **Peking Man**, from a site near Beijing. The fossils had been safely stored in the Cenozoic Research Laboratory at the Peking Union Medical College. But when Japan invaded China, the story darkens. The fossils disappeared, and there are several colorful legends as to what happened.

Some say the Marines helping in the evacuation were ordered to take "these boxes" on the train out of Shanghai with the evacuees headed for the United States. Supposedly the Marines even sat on the boxes on the train, not knowing what was inside.

There is also the possibility Japanese soldiers broke open the boxes, and when finding nothing but a bunch of old bones, tossed them on the ground where they were crushed by the crowds of people on the road to the ships.

Another story tells about a man claiming to have been one of those who unloaded the boxes upon arrival in California. He knew what was inside and buried the fossils somewhere in the Rocky Mountains near the west coast of California.

A Chinese official says the fossils weren't packed up for shipment to the United States until 1941 and that they disappeared en route to the port.

Another dubious tale has the bones going down with the Japanese freighter Awa Maru, which sank in 1945.

In 1972, a reward was offered for information as to the whereabouts of the fossils. Thirty-three years later, in 2005, the Chinese government founded a committee to find the bones or determine what had happened to them. They wanted the bones displayed on the sixtieth anniversary of the end of WWII. Japan was asked to cooperate, but declined. China wants the bones back, but the mystery surrounding the disappearance of **Peking Man** has now carried into the twenty-first century without solution.

With its troops in China now numbering over 350,000, Japan swept across the land, capturing the cities of Nanking and Shanxi by the end of 1937. It is believed about 300,000 Chinese were mass murdered in Nanking alone.

In 1939, Japan lacked sufficient males to man their growing military, so it conscripted Koreans, obviously against their will, to work in factories and mines in Korea and mainland Japan. Of the 5.4 million Korean conscripts, 670,000 were moved to Japan, which already had roughly 800,000 Korean immigrants living there. Some females were forced to work as "comfort women" for Japanese soldiers. Many Koreans were working in Hiroshima and Nagasaki factories when the cities were bombed. After the war, in an attempt to reconcile its mistreatment of Koreans during these times, Japan paid South Korea four billion yen and built a welfare center for Korean victims of the bombings.

Realizing it now controlled Shanghai, Nanjing, and most of northern China, the Japanese government decided to hold its horses, regroup, resupply, and then draw up a definitive plan to invade the Soviet Union. But its field generals were drunk with *sake* success and attacked the city of Taierzhuang, where Japan met its first defeat. Fighting back, Japan took the city of Wuhan, the site of the Chinese government. The Chinese were forced to retreat and set up a provisional capital in Chongqing (Chung King). Chiang Kai-shek's demand for Japan to withdraw to its pre-1937 borders was responded to by Japan launching an all-out air war, bombing civilian targets in almost every major city in China. China fought on, but by the time American Allies declared war on Japan in 1941, an estimated 20 million Chinese had been killed. This was the greatest slaughter of humanity in modern times.

During the 1930s, a growing unrest grew in many parts of the globe as countries challenged their neighbors. Germany invaded Poland and then annexed Czechoslovakia and Lithuania. After striking an alliance with Italy, Hitler convinced Italy to invade Ethiopia and Albania. In South America, Colombia and Peru fought a war in 1932-33, while Bolivia and Paraguay fought for three years starting in 1932. Spain's civil war involved participation by Germany, Italy, and the Soviet Union from 1936-39. The world was broiling with discontent and wars. People were unhappy with their governments, and their governments were unhappy with their neighbors. Travelers had to be careful where they went around the world for fear of finding themselves in the middle of a war zone. Nations didn't know who to trust. One day a neighbor was a friend, the next day they invaded your country.

In the United States, people were busy trying to climb out of the Great Depression, started by the stock market crash in 1929, and lasting ten horrible years. It ended in 1939 as we ramped up for war. There is no doubt all the work and jobs created in preparation for the pending war greatly helped pull the United States out of the Depression. But going to war should not be used as a solution to end any possible future depressions or similar economic downturns. To this day we continue to go to war against any country that doesn't run its country the way we think it should, and we continue to make enemies, not friends. Will Washington ever learn? War is not the answer to getting along with our neighbors around the globe. Switzerland and Brazil have not gone to war with anyone in over a hundred years. Result? They have no enemies.

In 1937, the Soviet Union continued to fan the flames of war in China in order to keep Japan from invading Siberia. It gave China a volunteer air force under the code name Operation Zet. Secretly, Soviet advisors offered $250,000 credit for munitions, war supplies, and the modernization of the existing Chinese airplanes. Over time, 3,000 Soviet advisors and pilots fought for the Chinese, and 227 died in the war. Within four years the Soviet support was replaced by the American Volunteer Group (AVG), better known as Commander Claire Chennault's *Flying Tigers*. American and Canadian-born Chinese, who had been trained by the Brits, infiltrated China with the mission to sabotage and destroy Japanese supply routes, such as bridges and railroads. They achieved some success in tying up the movement of Japanese forces, delaying their advances until Allied forces could martial other support and actions to stop Japan's further invasion of China.

Finally, the United States could no longer stand by and watch our Chinese friends be slaughtered by the Japanese. We, along with Great Britain and the Dutch East Indies, began an oil and steel embargo on Japan, making it impossible for it to continue fighting in China. This embargo was also the catalyst for getting the United States into the war, as Japan retaliated by attacking Pearl Harbor. Also in 1941, China finally and formally declared war against Japan, Germany, and Italy, and the world was once again at war. And yet today, Russia and Japan have not signed a formal peace treaty.

CHAPTER 2

BECKHAM FAMILY MOVES TO FLORIDA

Walter H. Beckham Jr. was born April 18, 1920, at his family's home in Albany, Georgia, at the end of WWI and the beginning of the Roaring 20s. He was the first of three sons born to Walter H. and Clara Octavia Beckham. His brother, Charles M. Beckham, died of polio at age twenty-nine. His youngest brother, Robert J. Beckham, is a partner in the law firm of Holland and Knight in Jacksonville, Florida.

Walter's family moved to Miami when he was five, drawn by word that people were waiting in line for lawyers to help them close real estate deals. But when the Great Depression came, his parents almost lost their home. They were forced to rent one of their rooms for additional income, and Walter worked part time in a butcher shop to help out. His mother's family had money, but his parents were not about to ask for help. They would manage as best they could with what they had. Walter remembers riding his bike along the small roads through the swamps and hummocks just south of Miami, in what he imagined as an African jungle. It was there that he hunted quail for the dinner table with his .22 caliber rifle. Throughout his schooling, Walter stood out. He was an honor student and athlete, the first in every category. He showed exceptional intellect and leadership abilities as early as when he attended Ada Merritt Junior High School. Walter had the whole package; he was a scholar and an athlete. He was the real deal and the envy of all the other boys. He was, already, the Big Man on Campus (BMOC), recognition typically not earned until one was in college. He lettered in baseball, was the manager of the football team, president of the student body, won the Boy's Scholarship Key, and won the American Legion Medal for boys, which was the highest award given to a graduating senior. It was no surprise the cute little girl who caught his eye, Ethel Koger (who later became his wife), matched his achievements by winning the American Legion Medal for girls. Having met Ethel, he never again needed to meet another girl. From that day on, and for the rest of his life, he was smitten. He only had eyes for Ethel; there never was anyone else. Such love for each other is sought by many, but found by few. Again matching achievements, they both served terms as president of the student body.

At Miami Senior High School, Walter excelled in tennis, baseball, and wrestling. He was a cheerleader, president of his Hi-Y and the State Hi-Y clubs, president of the student body, and winner of the Boy's Scholarship Award, the Damenstein Honor Student Award for service to the school, the Goldstein Medal, and the Pi Chi Cup. He also graduated valedictorian of his class. He and Ethel continued to be quite a team around campus. Never having a serious interest in any other girl, Walter declared his devotion to Ethel every year by reserving a date with her for New Year's Eve a year in advance. The tradition would continue throughout their lives, with the exception of the years he was away in the war.

When he and Ethel graduated from Miami Senior High School in 1937, Walter already reckoned Japan and Germany had a secret pact to attack and ultimately invade the United States from the west and east coasts simultaneously. With his penchant for planning ahead, one wonders if Walter envisioned what would happen when Germany and Japan met on either side of the Mississippi River. Having been partners to that point, might they attack each other in quest of owning all of the United States, or might they have drawn a line down the middle of the river, much as the Allied forces did in 1945, dividing East and West Germany? Fortunately, we will never know.

In the fall of that year, Walter was admitted to the College of Arts and Science at Emory University. While at Emory, he distinguished himself as a member of the Phi Beta Kappa, Omicron Delta Kappa, Eta Sigma Psi and Alpha Epsilon honor societies. He was president of the Chi Phi fraternity, vice president of the student body, member of the Executive Council of Emory Christian Association, undergraduate assistant in the history department, debate team coach, and varsity debater. He won the freshman tennis and wrestling tournaments, and was chairman of the Honor Council. To be labeled an overachiever was an understatement when referring to Walter.

In 1937, Walter entered college. He had been pre-ordained to attend Emory University, as today his family now spans three centuries of Emory graduates. (Walter's grandfather, Robert Young Beckham, was the first to attend Emory, followed by his youngest son, Walter's father, then Walter and his two brothers, Charles and Robert. Walter's three children, Barbara, Walter III, and James, as well as their maternal grandmother and uncle all graduated from Emory. The legacy continues with Walter's two grandsons, James's two sons.) When it comes time for anyone in the family to start thinking about college, the decision has already been made. The Emory blue and gold Eagles, and unofficial mascot Lord Dooley, always wins—hands down.

Four years later, he graduated with an AB degree with honors in American history. Walter had indeed heard the winds of war blowing out of Germany and Japan in the late 1930s. He was now starting to chart his own course in life, later telling his son, Walter III, *"It was just a matter of time before war broke out with Japan, so I knew I was going to be serving, and wanted to do so as an officer."* Walter was already a renaissance man.

THE WINDS OF WAR START BLOWING

In September 1940, the first Selective Training and Service Act went into effect, requiring men between the ages of twenty-one and thirty-five to register with their local draft board. Immediately following the attack on Pearl Harbor, in December 1941, a call to arms rang out across the country and the registration age was extended from eighteen to sixty-five; the draft age was extended from eighteen to forty-five. Thousands of Americans volunteered to join the military and fight for their country. Included in their numbers were hundreds of movie stars and professional athletes who willingly suspended their lucrative careers.

That same year, the United States Navy saw a need for massive construction projects to be built on foreign soil in order for the Navy to prosecute the pending wars in the Pacific and Atlantic theaters. The first problem was determining who would do the work, and under whose command. The Secretary of the Navy determined the new construction battalions would consist of construction workers drawn from the civilian workforce, not sailors, and they would be commanded by officers of the Civil Engineer Corps—further, they were to be called Seabees.

Realizing international law forbade civilians to resist enemy military attacks under penalty of execution as guerrillas, the Navy determined Seabees had to become enlisted men and officers of the Navy. The first recruits came straight from the men who built Boulder Dam, our national highways, and shipyards. Given age waivers up to age fifty (some were later determined to be sixty), they attended an abbreviated three-week boot camp where they learned basic military rules and regulations, and rudimentary use of small firearms. This was deemed necessary as they would often come under fire while carving out airstrips, docks, and bases on foreign soil, such as the islands of the South Pacific. Oftentimes, they worked alongside invading Marines as they clawed their way onto the islands under heavy opposition fire. The Seabees were building facilities to be used by Walter's future ship and all the other ships soon to arrive on station.

From the inception of the Seabee Battalions, the Navy required 400 advanced bases to be built, starting in the United States and reaching across both the Atlantic and Pacific oceans. The island chains became known as "roads." In the case of the Pacific, all roads led to Japan.

One example of Seabee construction was that of Naval Construction Battalion Detachment 1012, which built an airstrip, docks, and a base on the Galapagos Islands of Ecuador. Another site was that of the First Construction Battalion assigned to build a site for planes and ships to refuel on the island of Bora Bora, which carried the code name BOBCAT. The Seabees quickly identified with the name and called themselves "Bobcats." The name Bobcat evolved into the name given to a small bulldozer still used in construction today. Seabees assigned to the 1st Marine Division bulldozed paths through the jungle on Cape Gloucester so the Marine tanks could reach the Japanese positions on the island.

One of the many heroic acts by a Seabee occurred on October 2, 1942, on Guadalcanal. Not liking being shot at while he was working out in the open, Seabee Seaman 2d Class Lawrence "Bucky" Meyer simply picked up a machine gun and shot down a Japanese Zero that was strafing his fellow

Seabees. *"Take that you lousy Jap,"* Bucky shouted. Unfortunately, "Bucky" was awarded the Silver Star for his action posthumously, as he was later killed by enemy gunfire while working on a fuel barge on the other side of the island.

By the war's end, over 300,000 Seabees worked and fought in combat. 290 were killed in action, five received Navy Crosses, and thirty-three were awarded Silver Stars. Their contributions were an integral part of the U.S. Navy's victories in WWII.

On Christmas Eve of 1941, newly commissioned Ensign Walter Beckham, assigned to the Navy Supply Corps School, was attending Harvard Business School. Around that same time, General Douglas MacArthur, commander of all allied forces in the Philippines, realized he didn't have enough troops, beans, and bullets to withstand a pending mass invasion by the Japanese. As the battles took place on several different islands, the odds grew worse for the American and Philippine troops. The fighting was fierce, as food, clothing, barbed wire, gasoline, sandbags, and medicines became short in supply. Malaria, scurvy, and dysentery started taking a toll on the troops. The numbers of those physically able to fight were diminishing rapidly. If not killed by the Japanese, some were taken prisoner and burned alive on the island of Palawan. After several months of fighting, General MacArthur and the president of the Philippines, Manuel Quizon, were ordered to leave. Our main forces withdrew to Bataan and Army General Jonathan Wainwright replaced General MacArthur as commander of all the forces in the Philippines. Fight on as they did, on May 6, 1942, General Wainwright was ordered to surrender all allied forces in the Philippines to Japanese Lieutenant General Masaharu Homma. Lacking trucks to transport the 60,000-plus Filipino and allied prisoners to the nearest POW camp, the POWs were forced to get there by shank's mare. Thus began the eighty-mile Bataan Death March to the port city of San Fernando.

BATAAN DEATH MARCH

Among those troops were members of the 192nd Tank Battalion from Maywood, Illinois. Company B consisted of 122 young men from the 33rd Tank Company, 33rd Infantry Division of the Illinois National Guard. Company A troops came from Janesville, Wisconsin, Company C troops came from Port Clinton, Ohio, and Company D troops from Harrodsburg, Kentucky. All Company B troops grew up in Maywood and attended or graduated from Proviso High School. The Draft Act of 1940 called them to active duty. They left the Armory on the corner of Madison Street and Greenwood Avenue on November 25, 1940 amid a large crowd of families and friends who cheered and cried as they boarded a Northwestern Railroad train bound for the Pacific. After receiving additional combat training in California, 103 of them, along with their brand new M3 *Stuart* light tanks, arrived in the Philippines on November 20, 1941.

Bataan Death March Boxcar

In December, the 192nd combined with the 194th Tank Battalion to form the Provisional Tank Group assigned to launch a counterattack against the Japanese tanks in the first tank battle of the war. Company B, commanded by Captain Donald Hanes, was immediately weakened when there was no fuel for their tanks upon reaching the town of Gerona. Only one of the five platoons could actually continue to battle with the Japanese 4th Tank Regiment. Vastly outgunned by the Japanese Type 95 diesel-powered light tanks, Company B was ordered to protect the retreat toward the Bataan Peninsula. In no time, all five of Company B's tanks were destroyed by either the Japanese tanks or the Zeros attacking them from the sky. On April 8, the code word "Crash" was received, and all remaining tanks of the 192nd and 194th Tank Battalions were destroyed to prevent them from being used by the Japanese. On the following day, April 9, 1942, just one month after arriving in the Philippines, all United States and allied forces in the Philippines were ordered to surrender.

The first leg of the eighty-mile march was from Mariveles to Balanga, the capital of Bataan. From there, they were marched to the town of San Fernando and put on a train to the town of Capas. From Capas, they walked another nine miles to their internment camp, Camp O'Donnell. Many never made it to Camp O'Donnell. The Japanese were not equipped to handle this many prisoners, so their method of reducing the population to house and feed was to treat them inhumanly along the march. Many prisoners were already suffering from wounds in battle, yet they were beaten, bayoneted, shot, or otherwise mistreated along the way. Some were even beheaded by Japanese officers who were practicing using their swords while on horseback. There was no food or water for the first three days, and little after that. The only water offered was from the water buffalo wallows along the roadside. In one instance the guards offered "hot tea" to some of the prisoners. Several of the men stuck coconut shell cups under the bucket. As they gulped the first swallows they stopped. The guards were laughing as the prisoners realized the tea had a vile smell and taste. The guards had served them hot water laced with their urine.

The Japanese soldiers looked at the prisoners as subhumans because they believed no honorable soldier would ever surrender. They believed honorable soldiers committed *hari-kiri* before surrendering. Dysentery, insect bites, and other diseases were rampant. If a prisoner was too weak to go on, they were run over by trucks to finish the job of dying. If they were executed by guards, their fellow prisoners were ordered to bury their buddies by the side of the road or be executed themselves.

At San Fernando they were stuffed 100 or more at a time into small boxcars that measured a mere forty feet long and eight feet wide, with no ventilation, and no place to sit. The unbearable hot tropical sun took a further toll on their emaciated bodies. Even after arriving at Camp O'Donnell, the death rate was thirty to fifty per day. Most of the dead were buried in mass graves by Japanese bulldozers outside the compound. Later, those left alive were shipped to POW camps in Japan where the survivors were eventually released at the end of the war in 1945. Some died on board the hell ship that took them to Japan. Of the 103 men from Company B, none are known to still be living, four were rescued but their status is unknown, fifty-four died since the war, eight were killed in action, one is still listed as MIA, eleven died on board the hell ship, twenty-one died in prison camps, and four died as Japanese slave laborers.

Recently, Bataan Death March survivor Colonel Glenn Frazier told me his story:

On July 3, 1941, sixteen-year-old Glenn Frazier ran away from the cotton fields of rural Alabama to enlist in the U.S. Army. The immediate need was so great he shipped out to the Philippine Islands the following month before completing basic training. "You'll get it in the Philippines," he was told. Instead of basic training, he attended five months of ordnance school and was placed in charge of supplying ordnance to the front lines of the Filipino and American armies. He would load up his trucks during the day and deliver the shells, bullets, and other ordnance at night under the cover of darkness. On April 9, 1942, he and other American and Filipino soldiers were captured. As they were lined up to begin the march, Frazier and a buddy hatched a survival plan. They moved into the third row of POWs so they would be out of the reach of the Japanese guards wielding their swords from the left, and somewhat protected from the right, though only one row in. Either way, they felt their odds of surviving were far greater than if they were to walk in either of the outside lines. Starving and dehydrated, they were dizzy and disoriented under the scorching sun when they finally staggered into Camp O'Donnell. Of the original estimated sixty members of the 75th Ordnance Depot Company who began the march, Frazier and his buddy numbered among the twenty-five who made it. From O'Donnell they were shipped to POW Camp #1 in Osaka, Japan, where Frazier was assigned to slave labor duties seven hours a day. The prisoners were so malnourished and weak from various diseases and ailments, that the Japanese knew they couldn't work them longer hours or the prisoners would die. Breakfast was a small bowl of rice and soup, while lunch was rice, seaweed, and sometimes bread. Dinner consisted of rice and soup, fish every ten days, meat once or twice a month, and one vegetable, typically an onion or potato. After serving three-and-a-half years as a POW, Frazier and all other American service members were released when Japan surrendered on September 2, 1945. Frazier says his reason to survive was seated in his deep hatred for the Japanese, and his uncompromising determination not to let them defeat him morally. Today, Colonel Frazier can often be found at the USS Alabama battlefield park telling his story to visitors and autographing copies of his book Hell's Guest.

Since 1946, when a light tank replica of the type used by the 192nd Tank Battalion (which this author played on many times as a boy) was placed in Maywood Park, a Bataan Day parade and memorial service has been held every year. It is attended by people from across the country so these brave men and their sacrifices will not be forgotten. "Lest we forget" remains one of the most meaningful mottos that came out of WWII.

After the war, Japanese Lieutenant General Masaharu Homma, commander of all Japanese forces in the Philippines, was found guilty of crimes against humanity and executed by a firing squad in 1946. Generals Hideki Tojo (Prime Minister of Japan who gave the order to attack Pearl Harbor), Kenji Doihara, Seshiro Hagaki, Heitaro Kimura, Iwane Matsui, and Akiro Muto, along with Baron Koki Hiroa, were found guilty of brutal treatment of American and Filipino POWs and executed by hanging in 1948.

CHAPTER 3

WALTER GOES TO WAR

Having signed an "agreement" to serve with the Navy on May 10, 1941, Walter was now ready to chart another course in his life. Due to the exigencies of the services, some individuals were not required to complete officer candidate or basic school before being commissioned. Such was the case of Walter, who was "appointed" the rank of Ensign–Assistant Pay Master in the Naval Reserve effective May 26, 1941. To allow his future wife, Ethel, to be present at his commissioning, Walter did not take his oath of office until June 24, at the U.S. Naval Air Station, Miami, Florida. Assigned to the Volunteer Reserve unit for Supply Corps duties, he awaited further orders. Being a bit brash for a brand new junior officer, he requested his commanding officer allow him to complete his first year at Harvard Law School, where he had just been accepted, before being assigned to active duty. As was his normal approach to life, Walter had a plan and fully expected the Navy to cooperate with him. The response to his request came in the form of a telegram ordering him to report for a physical examination on July 16. After his exam, he was to report to the Navy Supply Corps School in Boston in conjunction with starting his first year at Harvard Business School (not law school) beginning September 25, 1941. Having passed all the hurdles to join the Navy, he received a $150 uniform gratuity on August 13 to purchase uniforms. Though everyone around him was surprised the U.S. Navy would allow a brown-barred ensign to tell them how he was going to serve his country, Walter accepted the orders in stride. It was, as

Walter's application to join
the Navy, 1941

he saw it, in conformance with his plan. He thought he was controlling his own destiny.

After only four months in the Business School, Walter received further orders. He was to be detached from Boston on February 27, 1942, and proceed to his assigned port at which a large heavy cruiser, the USS *Portland* (CA-33), may be…and then report on March 31 for duty as assistant disbursing and supply officer. Walter took a train to San Francisco and departed there on March 23 aboard the SS *Antigua*, a cargo ship owned by the United Fruit Company contracted to transport troops and fruit to the Pacific arena until the end of the war. Walter arrived in Pearl Harbor at 1400 on March 30, but the *Portland* wasn't there. Instead, he reported to the officer-in-charge at Fleet Weather Central, Ford Island, Oahu. He must have been thinking to himself, "How are we going to win a war if we can't even find one of our ships?"

In 1989, Walter described his first impressions of the war in a letter to former *Portland* shipmate Bill Vickrey.

In Walter's Words...

"I arrived at Pearl Harbor at the end of March, 1942, and spent March and April on duty as a Coding Officer at the Fleet Weather Central on Ford Island in the center of Pearl Harbour. Of course the battleships were still sunk all around Ford Island at their moorings at that time, and there was still much visible damage to the Army installation at Hickam Field. There was no doubt in the minds of anyone with whom I had contact on Oahu that the Japanese indeed did plan to come back and occupy Oahu. I can remember very well watching the B-25s being loaded onto the aircraft carrier, USS Hornet (CV-8), which was moored on Ford Island in preparation for the Doolittle Raid on Japan. The scuttlebutt at that time was that these planes were being ferried out to Wake Island to reinforce our forces there. Of course, when the Doolittle Raid was made known, all of us knew where the raid originated."

Commander of the U.S. Fleet, Admiral Ernest King, and Air Corps General Henry "Hap" Arnold, believed a twin-engine bomber could take off from a carrier deck, and chose the B-25B "Mitchell" bomber for the job. First, the planes had to be lightened for takeoff on the short runways by stripping them of everything removable, including the lower gun turrets and Nordic bombsights, which were replaced with handheld sights costing less than $1 each. Even the heavy fuel capacity was reduced, which precluded the planes from returning to the ship after the bombing raid. They would carry fuel only sufficient to reach the China coast after the raid. They were being sent on a mission from which they knew they would not return, at least in the immediate literal sense.

On April 2, 1942, sixteen B-25 bombers were loaded onto the deck of the *Hornet,* and the ship headed west out of Pearl Harbor. The operation was so secret the *Hornet* commanding officer, Captain Marc Mitscher, had no prior knowledge the planes were being loaded onto his ship, nor why. Vice Admiral William "Bull" Halsey's flagship, the *Enterprise,* would provide air cover for the operation. As the *Hornet* moved toward the designated launch site, some 400 miles east of the Japanese coast, it was spotted by Japanese picket boats patrolling the waters for any approaching enemy ships. Before the picket boats were sunk, they sent radio signal alerts back to the mainland. The *Hornet* and *Enterprise* were 600 miles from target, but the planes were scrambled and in the air in minutes. The pilots and crews knew they did not have an extra 200 miles of fuel on board. Just sixteen days after leaving Pearl Harbor, then-Lieutenant Colonel Jimmy Doolittle led sixteen B-25 Mitchell medium bombers, with crews of fifty-two officers and twenty-eight enlisted men, on a bombing raid of Japan, in retaliation for their attack on Pearl Harbor. All sixteen planes bombed their targets, and the plan was to head west, landing their planes somewhere in China, possibly on the beaches. When the raid was over, all the planes were lost, three crew died in the raid, and of the eight who were captured, three were executed. An estimated 250,000 Chinese were killed by the occupying Japanese Army in retaliation for helping the Americans escape capture. The raid was a success in that all the bombs fell on or near Tokyo, letting Japan know it wasn't invincible. The United States could hit Japan the same way Japan had to hit the United States. The Japanese had just awakened a giant bear.

Until the raid on Pearl Harbor, battleships were the biggest and most powerful weapon the U.S. Navy had at its disposal. They could pound enemy shores from thirty miles away prior to a land invasion or engage enemy battleships in a toe-to-toe battle for dominance. Aircraft carriers sailed in support of battleships.

The first experiment with aircraft carriers occurred in 1911 when the USS *Pennsylvania*, armored-cruiser number 4, was outfitted with a flight deck on its bow to test the feasibility of operating planes off of ships. The first real aircraft carrier, the USS *Langley CV-1*, saw service in 1922. She was actually a cargo ship, upon which a flat flight deck had been built many feet above the main ship's deck, running its entire length. She carried fifty-five planes and had four five-inch guns. But with the bulk of the Pacific fleet's battleships sunk or out of commission, the Navy saw the dawn of aircraft carrier warfare. The USS *Yorktown* and USS *Lexington* were the two aircraft carriers used in the first carrier battle between American and Japanese forces in the Battle of the Coral Sea. They were monsters, each carrying eighty planes and cutting through the water at thirty-four knots.

What Walter did not know was that the *Portland* was already at sea headed for the Battle of the Coral Sea. He would not board the *Portland* (named after the city of Portland, Maine) until May 28. Finally, he was going to see some action and prayed he would live to tell about it.

The *Portland* (affectionately and respectfully known to her crew of 621 men as "Sweet Pea") was one of the most decorated ships of WWII during battles, campaigns, and operations in the Pacific. Designated the lead ship in the third class of "treaty cruisers," she was built by the Bethlehem Steel Company in Quincy, Massachusetts, launched May 21, 1932, and commissioned February 23, 1933, (while Walter was in junior high). Long, at 673'5", with a beam of 66'1", and weighing in at 9,950 tons, she was fast with a top speed of 32.7 knots. Her four screws were turned by engines generating 107,000 horsepower

(SHP). Designed for air defense, her armament consisted of nine eight-inch 55 caliber guns, eight five-inch 25 caliber dual purpose guns, four 40mm anti-aircraft gun mounts of sixteen guns, twelve 20mm anti-aircraft guns, and two scout planes and catapults. She was one of the most powerful war machines afloat. The mission of cruisers and smaller destroyers was to serve as protective screening escorts surrounding the aircraft carriers, forming a battle group. Actually, it was the Japanese who first developed carrier battle groups, or task forces, known as *Kido Butai*. Until the Battle of the Coral Sea, the United States used several single carrier battle groups before expanding its actions to include several battle groups, which was in response to the Japanese, who deployed multiple battle groups as well. In war, each side endeavors to commit superior fire power as they attempt to defeat their enemy or opposing forces, which amounts to—*whatever gun they have, we need a bigger gun.*

By war's end, "Sweet Pea" had earned sixteen battle stars. Ensign Beckham was on board for six of them:

June 3–6, 1942
Battle of Midway

August 7–9, 1942
Guadalcanal-Tulagi Landings

August 23–25, 1942
Eastern Solomons (Stewart Islands)

October 26, 1942
Santa Cruz Islands

November 12–15, 1942
Third Battle of Savo Island

August 10, 1942–February 8, 1943
Capture and Defense of Guadalcanal

WALTER'S INTRODUCTION TO "SWEET PEA"

"We cleared the channel out of Pearl Harbor, passed the submarine nets, and headed out for the open seas. I realized that at last this was it. This was what I had longed for during my wait of two months on the beach. This was my opportunity to begin to give something of myself to my country, and my previous period of training had been but a prerequisite, the preparation for this hour. I had thought I was in the Navy during those months of indoctrination and schooling, but as I stood on the foc'sle and watched the island fade away behind me, I knew that up until this moment I had not really been a part of that brotherhood of the sea which is the United States Navy. The waiting had been tedious for stories about actions in the South Pacific to trickle into the harbor. I could not escape the impression that the ship for which I was waiting was involved in some of these actions. But I had waited, stood my communication watches, and inquired about my ship whenever ships came into the port.

Ensign Beckham aboard USS Portland

Two months after I arrived from San Francisco, I was still waiting, when one morning the planes from one of our carriers began to land on our field, and the scuttlebutt told us that a task force would soon arrive. As the force entered our harbor I stood entranced and watched the carrier come into her berth as a mighty mistress of the seas. Her crew manning the rail upon her flight deck presented an unforgettable and impressive scene. Finally, after others of the force having entered and moored, I saw the long, sleek lines of the cruiser which was to be my home for the next year.

Crew of the USS Portland

The next day I went aboard to assume my duties. This was also the time I learned all naval officers and sailors wore black shoes, while the naval aviators wore brown shoes to compliment [sic] their brown khaki uniforms. Such were the vagaries of the military. I was cordially received and welcomed by my supply officer, who had been expecting me for some time. The officers of the wardroom also received me kindly, and I quickly found that the ship was fortunate in having officers and men of the caliber and abilities as those who manned her. As I looked around the wardroom I saw stacks of letters, newspapers and magazines. This was the first mail which the ship had received in over two months, and all the ship's company, who were not on watch, were busily scanning the latest news from home. One of our lieutenants received some thirty copies of his local newspaper and carefully sorted them and packed them in his room. After we put to sea, each morning he would bring one of the papers to breakfast with him and proceed to read over the news which, by this time, was probably two months old. He would never fail to exclaim over a friend's marriage or some other item of local news however and his morning reading of the paper was a source of much amusement to us all.

Two days after I arrived on board, we were underway with the other ships of our force. It was on this morning that I was on the foc'sle watching the land fade into insignificance on the horizon. It was a warm, June morning with a glorious sun and a bright, clear sky. A strong breeze was blowing which whipped the deep blue of the Pacific into short choppy waves. Schools of flying fish scudded by on either side of the ship, propelling themselves with quick, sharp thrusts of their tails and spreading their long fins to catch all the breeze possible, thus prolonging their flight. My feelings were mingled as I realized security and safety were being left behind even as the land itself faded away. I had looked forward to this time since I felt that the Japanese had treacherously thrust this war down our throats, but now that I was actually embarked on what all of us believed would be a mission of war against the enemy, the reality set in that this was deadly serious business. This wasn't a game of cops and robbers.

These men with whom I was associated were already veterans since they had had a part in turning back the Japanese in the Battle of the Coral Sea. There was a certain look of determination in their eyes which can come only after men have seen other men make the supreme sacrifice for their country. Some call it "shell shock" or "thousand yard stare." What you call it matters not. The look in one's eyes after having looked death in the face is unlike any other facial expression. In the life of our country we have sent far too many troops to fight and die in other countries [sic] wars. When will Washington ever see the true downside to war? These men of the Portland had seen the aircraft carrier, USS Lexington (CV-2), in her death throes and had rescued 39 officers and 683 enlisted survivors until further transfer could be affected. Here was none of the bravado of unseasoned recruits. In its place was a quiet, deep resolution to see the job through to a successful conclusion. As in answering the call for World War I, they went over there, and won't be back until it's over, over there.

That first day was spent getting accustomed to the roll and pitch of the ship and was accompanied by that familiar queasiness in the abdominal region which most landlubbers experience when first putting to sea. Before we had cleared the channel I knew my place for abandoning ship, my battle station, and the place where my division came to its assigned positions for various other emergencies. There was an undercurrent of excitement on the ship as we found our course was, in general, northwest, for Japan lay in that direction and also certain of our possessions which were occupied by the Japanese. Also, more to the point in our thinking was the fact that Midway Island, our farthest vanguard in this area, lay near our course. There was much speculation as to our final destination and our mission. We were operating with a carrier task force, and it was a comforting sight to look over and see the carrier USS Yorktown (CV-5) which had been damaged in Pearl Harbor, but repaired sufficiently to get back into battle with her flight deck loaded with planes while others hovered over her in the air. I already knew of the great work done by these queens of the ocean in the Battle of the Coral Sea. They are stately in appearance, but their broods of fighting planes, dive-bombers, and torpedo planes remind one of a hornet's nest, which when disturbed, disgorges flight after flight of stinging retaliators.

We took up our position in the force which surrounded the carrier and began to steam steadily on our course. That evening we watched the carrier recover the planes that had been on scouting and antisubmarine patrols and prepare for the night. The undercurrent of excitement was increasing and continued during the next two days. As we proceeded north, the weather became much colder, and we encountered some mist."

Fighting battles at sea is much different from land battles. Not better or worse, just different. Radio communications, radar, sonar, intelligence reports, and scout planes are some of the methods used to find and identify an enemy that is constantly on the move. War ships don't anchor at night while the crew sleeps. They operate on three shifts of eight hours each, around the clock, maneuvering, often changing course to confuse the enemy. They are ever alert for a possible attack not earlier identified, one that could strike with bombs, torpedoes, or gunfire—from the air or another ship—and their first notice would come blaring over the ship's loud speakers, *"Now General Quarters… General Quarters…All hands man your battle stations…BONG BONG BONG"* on the bell, then General Quarters is announced a second time. Every officer and sailor knows exactly where his battle station is, and has seconds to get there. If the crew happened to be asleep in their bunks, oftentimes they would only take time to put on their shoes and trousers, along with their helmets, flak jackets, and life jackets. The ship's gangways and passageways were busier than Grand Central Train Station in New York City, with men running full tilt, bumping into each other, and not so much as a "by your leave, sir" or "brace"—what enlisted sailors normally called out when an officer was passing. This was no time for manners or protocol. This was war and they were rushing to kill or be killed. They would soon be fighting, bleeding, sweating, crying, praying, shouting profanities at an enemy who couldn't hear them, and writing messages of vengeance on torpedoes and bombs. Seeing unthinkable carnage on the decks of their ships, where many of the mangled and blown apart bodies were those of their fellow sailors and Marines, tore at their souls and inflamed their hearts with rage and hate. Many would die as they sought revenge for the horrible blow the Japanese had inflicted on the heart of the Pacific fleet moored in Pearl Harbor; a cowardly sneak attack, one in which they were not willing to meet on a field of battle to determine which side would win or lose. These members of the United States Navy were bent on exacting deadly punishment against an enemy undeserving of leniency or mercy. Walter's first battle was soon to come.

CHAPTER 4

MIDWAY

In all the annals of military history in the world, the Battle of Midway is one of the most defining hours. It was the most important naval battle of WWII, the turning point for the war in the Pacific. It has often been compared to England's King Henry V fighting in the Battle of Agincourt in 1415 during the Hundred Years' War. His message to his troops, before the battle began, was never written, but is memorialized in Shakespeare's play *Henry V.*

This day is called the Feast of Crispian.
He that outlives this day, and comes safe
home, will stand a tip toe when this
day is named…
We few, we happy few, we band of brothers;
For he today that sheds his blood with
me shall be my brother.
And gentlemen in England now abed
Shall think themselves accursed they
were not here, and hold their man hoods
cheap whiles any speaks that fought with
us upon Saint Crispian's Day.
Henry V October 25, 1415

Supreme commander of the Japanese combined fleet, Admiral Isoroku Yamamoto, was charged with annihilating the American fleet, first by striking its battleships in Pearl Harbor, and then making it an air war between the two country's carrier battle groups. What he didn't envision or imagine was that Midway Island was to be his Waterloo. He believed the United States had only two carriers available to fight, the USS *Enterprise* (CV-6) and the *Hornet*, as the *Lexington* had been sunk, the *Yorktown* was badly damaged, if not lost, and the *Saratoga* was being repaired on the West Coast. Yamamoto believed the United States would be defeated at sea and left with no defense against his advancing, island hopping navy/army forces.

What Admiral Yamamoto did not know about was the existence of the Nisei Secret Service. In November 1941, the U.S. Army opened a language school at the Presidio in San Francisco to add an additional capability to U.S. intelligence services, one of foreign language translators. Six thousand second-generation Americans of Japanese descent volunteered, some to avoid being placed in the concentration camps for Japanese living in America. One of the first tasks they accomplished with aplomb was to crack the Japanese naval code (JN-25), giving the United States advanced information on the movement and plans of the Japanese navy. These were loyal Americans who stood ready to fight alongside U.S. troops against an enemy with whom they shared an ancestral heritage. Not only did they serve as translators and interpreters, they fought on the front lines with U.S. Army, Navy, Marines, Army Air Corps, British, Australian, Canadian, New Zealand, Chinese, and Indian combat units, many earning the Combat Infantryman's Badge. Juxtaposed against the 110,000 Americans of Japanese extraction rounded up and interned in California, one wonders how the government knew which were loyal Americans and which were potentially dangerous, even spies. Today, Americans make the same mistake when they view every Muslims in America as an Islamic terrorist.

American Admiral Chester W. Nimitz, commander of the U.S. Pacific fleet, used information from the Nisei Secret Service to create an ambush for Admiral Yamamoto. Yamamoto had been seriously embarrassed by Doolittle's raid bombing Tokyo in retaliation for Japan attacking Pearl Harbor, and being defeated in the Battle of the Coral Sea. He planned to take Midway before U.S. carriers could get there to defend it and then use the island as a Japanese airbase. But we were listening to all Japan's communications and, based on the intelligence, Admiral Nimitz brought all the carrier battle groups he could muster, positioned them around Midway, and waited for the Japanese to attack. Midway was the watermark for the United States in the Pacific.

At 1230, June 3, 1942, a flight of nine B-17 bombers left Midway in search of a Japanese Tanaka transport group. Early the following morning, a torpedo from an American flying boat struck the Japanese oil tanker *Akebono Maru*. Two hours later, four Japanese heavy cruisers left their destroyer escorts to commence shelling Midway. Search planes, both Japanese and American, were launched in search of enemy ships, now known to be near. Soon after, Vice Admiral Noguma launched his first attack on Midway. At first light of dawn, Lieutenant Ady's patrol bomber/scout/search (PBY) located two carrier task forces heading toward Midway. Within minutes, Lieutenant Chase's PBY had spotted many planes heading toward Midway. Twelve minutes later, fourteen B-17 bombers proceeded to bomb the Japanese carriers, and four minutes later, at 0600, twenty-four F-2 and F-4 fighters were in the air to attack the Japanese battle group. The carrier *Yorktown*, escorted by the *Portland*, was ordered to launch a full strike attack on the Japanese fleet. Also in the air were members of Fighting Squadron TEN off the *Enterprise*, including one of the Navy's most famous pilots, then-Lieutenant William I. Martin. Martin was the first pilot to execute a night takeoff and landing (eventually, a record 440) off the big "E," which was later reclassified as a CV (N)-6, a night carrier. Earning a Silver Star for his actions, Martin eventually rose to the rank of vice admiral, finishing his remarkable career in the navy as commander of the Sixth Fleet in Gaeta, Italy and commander, Naval Striking and Support Forces, Southern Europe. After retirement, Bill Martin spent much of his time interviewing candidates for the Naval Academy. He truly enjoyed talking with these young folks and evaluating who did and did not exhibit evidence of the high character and leadership qualities his navy was looking for. He died in 1996 and is buried at the Naval Academy. In 2000, Martin was added to the Naval Aviation Hall of Honor. Only eighty naval aviators have been given such recognition and honor.

At 0700, Admiral Raymond A. Spruance, commander of Task Force 16, ordered all aircraft from U.S. carriers to attack. Within an hour, six *Avenger* fighter bombers and four B-26 bombers attacked the first of four Japanese carriers, the *Akagi*; fourteen B-17 bombers attacked the *Soryu*; sixteen Dauntless dive-bombers attacked the *Hiryu*, and twelve more attacked the *Haruna*. The skies were full of planes shooting at each other and bombing ships, anti-aircraft guns from the ships were firing at the planes, and the biggest air war of WWII was underway.

The cacophony was deafening, leaving ringing in the ears for hours, as the smoke from burning ships darkened the sky—benefiting and hiding both Japanese and American planes. The battle raged around the clock for four days. The *Yorktown* took three direct hits from the *Hiryu* dive-bombers, only to be hit again by two more torpedoes. Early in the morning on the fifth of June, Marine pilot Major Lofton Henderson led a flight of sixteen planes off the *Saratoga* in a bombing attack on the *Hiryu*. As he began his final run, his left wing was hit and exploded in flames. Henderson kept firing at the *Hiryu* until he crashed into the ocean very near the *Hiryu* and was lost at sea. Within hours the *Hiryu* sank. Planes were taking off and landing on the carriers' decks as fast as the flight control tower and deck crews could launch them. The noise of planes' engines, firing of guns coming from every direction, pounding of the cruisers' and the destroyers' big guns, crews hollering at each other for "medical assistance" and "more ammo" rang in everyone's ears. Sailors constantly rearmed the planes and guns. Hands were burned handling hot shells and guns. Grease, sweat, and black smoke darkened their faces, hands, and arms. Real sleep would not come until the skies were quiet. On the morning of June 6, the *Mogami* took four direct hits, and the *Asashio* was hit once. The Americans were gaining the upper hand. The battle was starting to go their way. That afternoon, more planes from the *Hornet* attacked the *Mogami* scoring a direct hit on its deck, preventing any planes from taking off or landing. The *Mikuma* is abandoned and sinks. Early in the morning of June 7, the *Yorktown* turned over on her port side and sank with all her battle flags flying. After the battle, Henderson received the Navy Cross posthumously for his actions. He was the first Marine aviator to die during the Battle of Midway. The island Lunga Point Honiara Airport is renamed Henderson Field in his honor.

WALTER'S FIRST TEST UNDER FIRE

"I was becoming accustomed to my quarters where I was the lowest man in a three decker bunk arrangement. The bunks were so close together that it was necessary to get into a prone position before attempting to enter mine. I was

sharing a state-room with four other ensigns, one of who had come aboard on the same day as I. On the first morning at sea, I had come wearily out of my bunk as General Quarters sounded well in advance of daybreak, and saw what was to be the first of many, many sunrises at sea. It is a beautiful and inspiring sight to see the sun spring out of the ocean after a forewarning of pink and gold in the first glow of morning. It is also a most welcome sight after the blackness which is night at sea in wartime.

The day of action dawned without bringing us any premonition of the events which were about to transpire, although we knew that we were due for action of some sort very soon. It was a beautiful day. The sun was bright, and the visibility was good. Our force was proceeding on its appointed course. Another of our forces was standing by at not too great a distance. Our scouting planes took off and began to make their search. The morning went by uneventfully. Shortly after the noon meal, however, we went to battle stations. The report came to us that our scouting planes had sighted a large enemy force near Midway. Immediately we could see the carrier agog with preparations for launching her planes, and it was only a matter of a few minutes before she turned into the wind and launched her first search and attack group. The aviators circled our force slowly as they came into formation. The bombs and torpedoes fastened to the bellies of the heavier planes could easily be seen as we watched from our ship. The fighter planes rose swiftly above the others, forming a protective screen. After the formation was complete and the final circle of salute to the force had been made, the air armada turned its back upon us and headed for the enemy. As they disappeared over the horizon, we entered a period of suspense which would only be broken by the report of the success or failure of their mission. Our tension mounted as time passed by with no word of our planes, and we were constantly on the alert to repel any attack which might materialize on our force.

Around three o'clock in the afternoon, our force was electrified by the report that enemy planes were approaching us. My battle station, at this time, was the ship's coding room, where I was attired in the customary battle dress of helmet and flash proof clothing. I had my life jacket lying close by. I felt a mixture of uneasiness and excitement since this was to be my first action. I did not see the first attack which was delivered by Japanese dive-bombers, though I could hear the roar of our guns as they sent up a barrage of steel around the carrier, which was the focal point of the attack. The attack itself lasted only a matter of several minutes, and it did not seem likely that much damage could have been inflicted on our ships in such a short time, but I was still a stranger to the sudden destruction that aircraft can bring. Finally the noise of the guns ceased. It was followed by what, in comparison, seemed an unreal quiet. I removed the cotton from my ears which had been protecting them from the noise and concussion, and ventured out on the weather deck. I was surprised and dismayed to see a thick column of black smoke pouring from the stack of the Yorktown, and it was motionless in the water. I learned from the men who had been on deck during the attack that she had been hit, and one of the bombs had gone down her smokestack into her fire and engine rooms. The smoke continued to pour out of her, and she remained dead in the water like some wounded animal.

Other ships came steaming over the horizon, and we recognized them as our own. They were coming to help us guard the carrier, since they had been informed of our plight. They came into line with us, and we circled the larger ship until her engineers were able to get her underway again. Then we resumed our battle line. When she was underway again, she launched additional planes. Shortly after this, we received reports that torpedo planes were coming in to attack us. The carrier, by this time, had gained some speed, and the other ships of the force were gathered around her so as to give the maximum gun coverage in case the attack centered on her again. Our position was astern of her. Just prior to this time, the ship's communication officer had given me some dispatches which were to be delivered to the Captain, and I proceeded to the bridge. As I arrived there the torpedo planes appeared on the horizon off our port beam. We could see some of them falling in clouds of smoke but others continued to advance through the protective ring of fighter planes and gunfire that was between them and us. I stood transfixed on the bridge. I was cold, and I was scared as I watched those six or seven Japanese torpedo planes approach our formation and prepare to launch their deadly missiles at us. All of our anti-aircraft guns were firing, and the noise and concussion were terrific. The sky was dark with the burst of five inch gunfire, and the tracers of the smaller caliber guns crisscrossed in a crazy pattern all around the torpedo planes. But they came right on in through our barrage, looking like some giant birds that were not to be foiled in their search for prey. It seemed almost impossible that these planes could continue to advance through this hail of steel with which we ringed our force, but they came on toward us. Four or five of them were grouped together some fifty to a hundred feet above the water. Another was alone and below the rest. They headed directly for the carrier Yorktown. She was blasting away with all her guns and turning to try to avoid them. As I watched, a sickening feeling came over me. The shrapnel bursts and the clouds of smoke from the gunfire were bewildering, and most of all, these planes were a bit terrifying as they seemed to hang in the sky in spite of all our frantic efforts to blot them out. They came in and dipped down for their torpedo runs on the carrier, and I watched in awe as I saw three of the planes launch their torpedoes which hit the water with a little splash and then proceeded on their deadly mission. We were directly behind the carrier and as two of the torpedoes hit; I could see her list heavily to the port side. The list became greater and greater as the water rushed into the great holes torn open by the torpedoes. As I watched, one of the Japanese planes came across the bow of our ship, did a vertical bank, and turned to leave the scene. The large orange colored rising sun could plainly be seen on the underside of the wings. It was different from anything that I had ever seen before, and it looked incredibly large. This plane and the others never returned to their ships, however, for the gunfire and fighter planes accounted for all of them.

Turning my gaze from the planes, I looked at the wounded Yorktown which was lying dead in the water again, and listing so heavily to port that her hangar deck seemed to be almost touching the water. One of her planes which had been on the flight deck had slid across and was hanging over the side. At this time, a signalman sent word up to our bridge the order to abandon ship had been given on the carrier. I borrowed a pair of field glasses from one of the other officers standing nearby, in order to see more clearly what was happening. I could plainly see some of the men climbing down the long ropes suspended from the sides of the ship and sliding off into the water, while others plunged directly from the deck into the sea. All seemed to be clad in life jackets. They looked as if they were ants as they clambered down the sides of the ship. The other ships in the force, including our own, began a protective circling movement around the distressed ship. The destroyers went in close to pick up the survivors who were swimming and floating in the water. There was no panic among the survivors as the skippers maneuvered their ships into position in order to get the men out of the water as soon as possible.

In the meantime, some of our planes had returned from their mission and were not able to land on the carrier. Therefore, they proceeded to another carrier which was not too far a distance and which had not been damaged by the Japanese. A few of our pilots refused to leave the scene and remained in their fighter planes over our formation in case the Japs should come back for the third time. These men stayed over us until their gasoline supply was exhausted, then parachuted down into the water or crash landed their planes, taking a chance on being able to be rescued by the destroyers. It is impossible to pay too high a tribute to the Navy and Army Air Corps pilots who were willing to make such sacrifices."

As suddenly as the thunderous noises of the attack took place, the sounds grew silent as if directed by a band leader's baton. The guns stopped firing, the planes flew away back to their carrier homes, fires were put out, the skies slowly cleared of smoke pushed away by the prevailing winds, survivors in the water were rescued, horns and sirens stopped blaring, crews stopped hollering and running on decks, gangways, and below decks, and all became quiet. Exhausted, they just sat where they were, lit up a cigarette, looked around to see who was still alive and effectively okay, and reflected on how they had cheated death once again. Their world slowed down as the ringing in their ears subsided, and their thoughts went from the battle to their loved ones back home on the farms and in the towns and cities of the good ole US of A where they grew up and worked—what seemed like so long ago. Then reality crept back in and they started wondering when the next attack would come. *"Best we go down below, wash some of the grime off, and try to catch some sleep while we can,"* occupied their minds. The uncertainty of when "**MAN YOUR BATTLE STATIONS**" would again sound made them write brief letters home because it may be their last. Who knew when a shell or bullet out there had their name on it? War takes many tolls on the body and mind, which cannot be calculated or prepared for. It's something they just had to endure.

In Walter's Words...

"We expected to be attacked again; not realizing the terrific damage which our planes had inflicted on the enemy, but another attack never came that day. This was the Battle of Midway as we saw it from the decks of a cruiser, and not until later, did we know the heroic achievements of the aviators whom we had seen take off in the search and attack groups. For many of them, that was the last takeoff, but we shall never forget the deeds which they performed.

Our ship was designated to take the survivors from the destroyer USS Hamman (DD-412), which had been sunk while trying to assist the sinking Yorktown, since we were one of the larger ships present. That afternoon, one of the destroyers came alongside us and preparations were made to affect a transfer. However, at this time, another destroyer reported a submarine contact, and we immediately cast off the lines and postponed the transfer until the next day. It was now late afternoon and the sun was beginning to set. Our force left several destroyers around the Yorktown to protect her, and we began to steam eastward.

This was the end of the action for us, but other forces remained and concluded the task of achieving the greatest naval victory we had ever scored and the first real defeat for the Japanese Navy in over three hundred years.

I shall never forget my feelings as we left that spot in the late afternoon. The last sight which we ever got of the Yorktown as she fell astern was a memorable one. She stood as a silent, solitary sentinel in a wilderness of water. Alone and abandoned except for her escort, she awaited her fate. She still had a list to port, but she was still afloat, and hope rose in us that she could be towed into port and repaired. This was the last we ever saw of the gallant Yorktown."

On June 4 and June 11 respectively, Commander W. B. Coleman, the executive officer of the *Portland*, submitted an action report to the commanding officer of the *Portland*, Captain Laurance Toombs DuBose, and Captain DuBose submitted a more detailed after action report to the commander, Pacific fleet, Admiral C. W. Nimitz. These reports provide the most complete description of the part the *Portland* played in the Battle of Midway. (See copies at addendums 1 and 2.) These documents were declassified by the Navy Department in 1968.

The United States won the Battle of Midway, beating a Japanese Navy that had not lost a battle in 300 years, but there was a terrible cost shared by both sides:

United States losses:
- 1 carrier—*Yorktown*
- 1 destroyer—*Hamman*
- 145 aircraft
- 307 men

Japan's losses were far greater:
- 4 carriers—*Akagi, Hiryu, Kaga* and *Soryu*
- 1 cruiser—*Mikuma*
- 5 ships damaged—cruiser *Mogami*, destroyers *Arashio* and *Asashio*, oiler *Akebono*, destroyer *Tanikaze* and battleship *Haruna*
- 292 aircraft
- 2,500 men

In Walter's Words...

"That night was spent hashing and rehashing the events of the day wondering how much damage we had done to the Japanese to make up for the damage they had done to us. I was very excited and still a little sick over all I had seen during the day. The vision of those men going overboard after their ship had been given a death blow still haunted me. I slept uneasily and was glad when morning came."

After a battle the scout planes take on another role, that of searching for survivors. On June 7, one of the *Portland's* scouts, a Curtiss SOC-1 Seagull, number 10, piloted by Lieutenant JG Ralph "Kaiser" Wilhelm, helped find survivors of the *Yorktown* who were later brought on board the *Portland*.

USS *Portland* Seagull scout plane searching for downed flyers, June 7, 1942, Battle of Midway

In Walter's Words...

"We spent all the next day in taking survivors aboard from the destroyers. They came alongside one at a time, and by the use of a bo'sun's chair, the survivors were transferred from the rolling decks of the smaller ships to ours. The bo'sun's chair consists of a long line which is strung between the two ships on which the chair (for a person) or bag of material is hung.

There is a light line strung from each side of the chair or bag, which enables it to be pulled from one ship to another. The men are placed in the chair on one ship, and then pulled across the intervening water by men on the other ship. The empty chair or bag is then pulled back to the transferring ship where it is reloaded and the process repeated. Several "chairs" can usually be kept running at the same time, and thus a fairly speedy transfer of a considerable number of men or material can be accomplished in a reasonable period of time, so long as the seas cooperate. One of the most common exchanges accomplished in this manner is the exchange of movies. Except during combat operations, a movie is shown every night on the ship's mess deck, and there are only so many nights a movie can be reshown before an exchange is made with another ship. A good movie is one of the few entertainments available to the crew when out at sea. Another is the infrequent "smoker" when boxing and wrestling matches are held on deck, oftentimes involving the settlement of a disagreement between sailors and/or Marines on board.

We began receiving the men shortly after sunrise and it was late afternoon before the task was completed. The men from the Yorktown were glad to get back on a larger ship, as many of them had been forced to sleep on deck the night before, and not being used to the increased rolling and pitching of the smaller ships, had become sea sick. Also, they had been wet and many of them had very little, if any, clothing. Even considering the great generosity of the destroyer crews with their own shoes and clothing, there still was not enough to go around. As soon as some of the survivors had been transferred, if they were not wounded or sick, they were put to the job of helping pull their comrades across. This accomplished the two-fold good of relieving our own ship's crew, thereby enabling them to continue with their own work, and also keeping the survivors busy, which was the best thing for them. They turned to this job with considerable enthusiasm. Two lines were formed—one for those with shoes and one for those without, so those with shoes would not hurt those without. Each newcomer would take his place at the rope until he worked his way to the end of the line, then he would leave and let those who had come over after him to continue the task. Each line was directed by a bo'sun's mate who gave his directions by means of prearranged signals on his pipe whistle. The shrill blast of the pipe could be heard throughout the day as the transfers were completed.

The wounded were transferred in stretchers which were hung from the ropes and upon arrival on board they were immediately taken to our sick bay, where they were put to be cared for. Many of them had shrapnel wounds or burns and were in considerable pain. They were somber as they remembered their ship, the fate she suffered, and the many shipmates who had been lost, but already they were talking about their willingness to get back on her if she could be saved, and about returning to take another shot at the Japs. The ship's company helped in every way possible to find these men suitable clothing and some sort of shoes, and before long, they were fairly well outfitted. Best of all, with the facilities of our larger galley, we were soon able to give them a large hot meal which did more to revive their spirits than about anything else that could be done.

Another officer came to me with a large sum of money in his hands. He told me he had been the treasurer of the Officer's Mess and that just before abandoning ship he had gone to his room and grabbed all of the mess funds that could conveniently be reached, and stuffed it in his pockets. When he brought me the money it was soaking wet. Therefore, our first act was to take the money to the ship's laundry where we pressed it dry. I shall never forget the expression on the laundry operator's face as he saw the first thousand dollars put on the presser to dry. I then put the money in my safe where I kept it for him until he left the ship.

In the afternoon, one of the destroyers which had pulled alongside us and transferred some men also took from us some of the technical men who had been transferred from other destroyers. Scuttlebutt was this ship was taking a skeleton crew back to the injured carrier so they could aid in getting her into port. Truth being, the destroyer was alongside the carrier when it was later torpedoed by a Japanese submarine and both ships were sunk. War is forever bringing home to us all the uncertainty of the future and of life itself. That night the men were sleeping all over our ship and hardly an empty space on deck could be found. The ship was literally bulging with men.

Some two or three days later, we retransferred our survivors to a large submarine tender USS Fulton (AS-11) which was to finally carry them back to Hawaii. The process of the bo'sun's chair was repeated and the transfer took several hours. By this time, we were well out of the battle area and were ourselves on the way back to port. Other of our forces had remained at Midway to finish the job which we had helped begin and for us the Battle of Midway was a closed chapter in our war careers. I was now a veteran and I found that I was universally accepted as a shipmate. Before the battle, they had all been kind and friendly, but now the feeling was deeper and I was considered one of them. There is a difference, as any man who has served on one of our fighting ships in this war will testify.

The greatest single factor that had impressed men in this battle had been the morale of our men. In the face of crisis, they were calm and deliberate and I had read the resolution and determination in the faces of the survivors. The good nature and morale of the American sailor is indeed a tribute to the Naval Service of our country. It never shows more plainly than when confronted by an intense and challenging situation. I was to realize this even more fully in the days to come."

What Walter and even the U.S. Navy did not know at the time of the Battle of Midway was that Japan had a secret weapon they were planning to use on the Panama Canal. Most of our troops and supplies sailed from the East Coast through the Canal, the gateway to our forces in the Pacific.

Early in 1942, Admiral Yamamoto ordered eighteen I-400 series submarine/aircraft carriers built. He envisioned this to be the weapon of choice when he was ready to attack the U.S. mainland. They dwarfed any submarine we had in the water at the time, and could sail around the world one and a half times without refueling, enveloped in paint completely undetectable by sonar. Their most potent weapon was a trio of *Aichi Seiran* seaplanes armed with torpedoes and 1,800 pound bombs. The planes' wings folded back alongside the fuselage as they were loaded one in front of the other inside a tube that reached from the deck down into the sub. The plan was that when the sub reached its destination, the planes would be catapulted into the air. They would fly to their target, using radar that would detect any enemy planes up to forty miles away, drop their torpedoes/bombs, and return alongside the sub. A crane then lifted them back on the sub and they disappeared into the tube.

On June 21, 1942, an early version of the I-400 bombed Vancouver Island in Canada, followed the next day by another one that bombed Fort Stevens in Oregon. What Admiral Yamamoto understood was North America was heavily forested from coast to coast, and he knew the prevailing winds always blew west to east. He reasoned incendiary bombs would ignite fires in the forests on the West Coast and burn all the way across most of Canada and the United States. Fortunately, the Vancouver and Fort Stevens bombings caused only small fires that were easily distinguished. Then on February 24, 1943, Yamamoto bombed an oil refinery in Santa Barbara, California. Now he had the United State's attention, but the Americans did not yet know where the bombs originated. Completing these operations, Yamamoto inexplicably decided to scale back his fleet from eighteen to five.

Japanese engineers had been working at the Canal since before the war, and presented Yamamoto with detailed blueprints of the locks into the Canal. The Mira Flores locks on the Pacific side were more vulnerable, but greater damage could be done on the Atlantic side's Gatun locks. Closing the Gatun locks to repairs for six months would have had dire consequences on the prosecution of the war in the Pacific, and might even have caused the United States to lose. But it took too long to set the trap. On August 12, 1945, two subs were stationed off the coast of Ecuador waiting for a third to arrive. The third sub was too late; V-J Day occurred three days later as a result of the bombings of Hiroshima and Nagasaki. The Navy was ordered to sail/tow two subs from Ecuador and three from Japan to Hawaii where they were used for target practice and then sunk. The general belief was the scuttling was necessary in order to prevent the Russians from having access to the subs under the Lend-Lease Program. Today, using the Japanese I-400 technology, the U.S. Navy launches missiles, instead of planes, off its submarines.

CHAPTER 5

STAND-DOWN

Walter and the rest of the crew of the *Portland* were standing down for an unknown period of time. In war, an unknown period of time is often short-lived.

Here Is What Walter Had to Say About It...

"We arrived in port several days later, and it was only then, when we could read the newspaper accounts of the stunning defeat that had been inflicted on the Japanese in our recent campaign, that we comprehended the scope of the operations in which our force had been involved. After arriving, we moored alongside a tender and her personnel immediately began to work on our ship in order to make the many necessary repairs. We were granted liberty from time to time and things were again quiet and peaceful. It seemed as though it would continue this way for some time as the days passed and we remained in port. It was restful and soothing to go ashore and relax again and everyone capitalized on his opportunity. Several very successful parties were given for the enlisted men. This was the first real rest the men had had in several months and it had a decidedly good effect on them. They were in need of rest and relaxation after the two strenuous campaigns in which they had participated.

We received and sent mail regularly, which is always a great morale booster. Also, it was nice to have new movies on board in the evenings, recently exchanged with other ships. Speaking of movies, it is a wonderful thing to watch the simplification of tastes which takes place after a month or two at sea. It no longer matters who is in it or how old the movie is. Nearly everyone who is not on watch attends when possible. Musical comedies are among the most popular and one of the first things done upon arrival in port is to send the movie officer in search of the best films available. Sometimes there are two runs so that one group may attend before going on watch, then the group coming off watch can see the second show.

In the late afternoons, after the evening meal and before evening colors and the movie, many of the younger officers would gather on the Foc'sle and talk while enjoying the sunset. As always, the talk was of home and their wives, sweethearts and families. Also, the latest scuttlebutt concerning when we might return to the States was repeated and weighed by all. Sometimes bets would be laid that we would be in the States by a certain date.

Early in July we left port suddenly for several days of gunnery drill, which included some shore bombardment drills. This gave rise to much speculation concerning our next mission. After the drills, we returned to the harbor, however, and waited in expectation of getting underway again very soon.

Early one morning, the word was passed over our speaker system to stand by to unmoor, and we knew then that the awaited time had come. Of course, our destination was unknown. But we were going back into battle that was for sure. We left our moorings and as we looked toward the mouth of the channel, we could see the carrier USS Wasp (CV-7), with which we were to operate already passing out into open sea. Soon our entire task force was in formation, having successfully cleared "torpedo junction," as the mouth of the harbor was jokingly called, since Jap submarines were sometimes lurking there, waiting for our ships to come out. Once again, we were to be a part of a carrier task force, and we were certain that we were again embarked on a mission which would result in damage to the enemy. This time, however, our course was in a southerly direction, and before we had settled down for our first night out, many possible objectives had been named by the members of our crew. Being mid-July, it was very warm, and even with the aid of our blower system, it was uncomfortably hot below decks at night, since all openings were closed when everything had to be blacked out. The heat increased as we proceeded further south and approached the equator. The sea was quiet and only the steady hum of our engines and a gentle roll reminded us that we were underway when we were off watch and turned in to sleep. As we came closer to the equator, I was forcibly reminded by the shell-backs on board, who had previously crossed the Equator, that I was at best only a lowly Pollywog, who had not yet "crossed the line" at sea. Though all formal initiations into the Ancient Order of the Deep had been suspended on most of our warships for the duration of the war, there was still a messy formal Pollywog initiation which few escaped on board ship. This consisted of a thorough butchering of the hair on one's head until the only alternative was to have one's head practically shaved. I had never really appreciated my head of hair until it was taken from me and I found that it takes about five months to have it fully grow back. Our fellow members of the wardroom took care of the officers, and the crew effectively trimmed its newcomers the night we crossed the invisible navigational line that separates the northern and southern hemispheres of the globe. The next day, we presented a bedraggled sight when we were forced to remove our hats.

As we entered southern waters, the Southern Cross had risen higher and higher in the sky. I had never seen this constellation before, but before I was to leave its domain, I was to become very familiar with it. When you are at sea, the stars assume a new meaning. At night when you sit on the foc'sle, or see them while on watch, it is like seeing and talking with old friends. They make you seem nearer to the folks you have left behind as you realize that some of these same stars will be shining on them.

The hot weather continued after we crossed the equator, maybe even growing hotter. The sea remained calm and peaceful, however, and a balmy breeze made it fairly comfortable on deck. One morning, we sighted an island ahead of us, and since it was the first island we had sighted since leaving port, we were very interested to know which island it was. As we approached, we could see it was ringed with coral reefs and was very flat, as are many of the islands of the South Pacific. We made our approach in the mid-morning *while our planes and destroyers maintained an anti-submarine patrol above and around us. I was greatly interested in the land which we were approaching, since my father had earlier instilled much of the sightseer instinct in me, and anything which was new and different fascinated me. Some of our men had been in this port before and they entertained us with accounts of the place, which included something of its people, vegetation, etc. It took some little time to get our entire force inside the reefs and into the harbor. When we were inside, we saw that there were several transports and cargo ships already present. A large red cross on a background of white identified another one of our ships present as being a hospital ship.*

Some of us were hoping to get ashore, but our hopes were rudely shattered as we soon found out we were only stopping here to refuel, and then push on. We came alongside a tanker shortly after we entered, and immediately the lines were thrown across and secured, and they began to fill our 1,600-ton fuel tanks. The other heavier ships were similarly engaged. After the heavier ships had refueled, the smaller ships came alongside the tankers for the same purpose. In the meantime, I had borrowed a pair of field glasses and had scanned the shore, which was not too far distant. I could see a crowd of natives inside some of the coral reefs, who appeared to be fishing with nets. They had a small horse or donkey with them and appeared to be wearing light clothing which they wrapped around themselves. A group of buildings projecting above the foliage marked the only sizeable settlement on the island. One place, which resembled one of our large residential homes, stood out from the others. The old timers on board told us that this was the home of the Queen who ruled this and several other islands, which were not far distant.

As soon as our ships had refueled, we immediately got underway. This time, five or six of the transport and cargo ships also got underway and accompanied us. This led us quickly to the conclusion we were part of a convoy which was to be protected by our combatant ships. Passing by us so close, we could see they were packed with men. And these men were United States Marines. Our force now consisted of some twelve to fourteen ships. We deployed as soon as we got into the open sea and by nightfall we were well on our way to battle again. The carrier and the merchant ships were in the center, surrounded by the destroyers and cruisers, which formed the escort. We continued in this formation for several days on our southern and westerly course.

During this time, the carrier held practices for the aviators aboard. One of these was held one afternoon when I was off watch and I had an opportunity to observe it. The carrier divided its force of planes into one protecting group and one attack group. The attack group was launched first and was to leave, then return, and attack our force, while the protecting group was to prevent the attack. Things were quiet for about an hour after the attack group left us, then suddenly out of the clouds the fighters of the attack group appeared and began to do a mock strafing attack on our ships. Our gunners followed them with their guns and thus derived some practice though, of course, no shots were fired by either force. I can well understand the confusion that a strafing attack can cause the enemy after watching our aviators deliver a mock one. The speed with which the fighter planes dive on the ships is almost incredible and it is exceedingly difficult to follow them with any precision. One of them came so close it looked as if he would hit our mainmast as he skimmed over us. At this time, the protecting fighter planes had found the attacking torpedo plane formation and had technically liquidated it, so we did not suffer a mock attack. These practice sessions are beneficial to the pilots, gunners and those maneuvering the ships, as they are entertaining to the rest of us. It is also a comforting feeling to know the planes are friendly as you see them diving and zooming around you.

As yet, we did not have any idea as to the mission, which was to be forthcoming, and it seemed entirely possible we might be taking reinforcements to some of our troops. We were soon to know differently, however, and to realize that our mission was offensive. This was projected into our thinking on the day of our rendezvous with other ships. One of my storekeepers came below to the office where I was working and told me a great number of ships had been sighted on the horizon. I immediately went topside to the weather deck and took a look around. It seemed that ships were lining the horizon all around us and my wonder grew as they continued to come into sight."

WRITING HOME

The abiding love Walter and Ethel had for each other during the war years is best evidenced by two poems they exchanged during those difficult times of separation. On May 20, 1942, Walter wrote:

A PRAYER

Each night I kneel in silent prayer

And pray "O" God, watch o'er her there.

Let courage surge within her breast;

Grant unto her Thy peace and rest.

Send faith to lead her, hand in hand

Up to Thee, For within Thy hand

There is no sorrow or despair

Since naught but hope do angels bear.

Kind Father, keep that smiling face

E'er before my eyes. There it's place

Must ever be in times of strife,

To bring new strength into my life.

O Grant that happiness may dwell

Within her soul and not that hell

Of pain and tears which war has wrought

As countless lives with blood it's brought.

Then head bowed low; on bended knee

I beg of Him beseechingly,

Until again men can be free,

Dear God, Please God, keep her for me.

Ethel's response is dated August 5, 1942:

A Tear

In uniform you looked so bold,

I caught my breath there in the cold.

Had all this horror and despair

Changed my loved one—in spite of prayer?

In silence there I prayed again,

Please let his tenderness remain,

The little things I loved him for

Please let them be there as before.

And then you caught my eye—and dear

The tenderness showed thru a tear.

GUADALCANAL

"Coyote is always out there waiting,
and Coyote is always hungry."
Navajo Indian saying

For the Marines on Guadalcanal and Iwo Jima, these battles were their defining hours, unlike any others. The few, the proud, the Marines stood tall and took these islands one foot at a time from the Japanese, who believed beyond any doubt they couldn't be taken.

By the summer of 1942, Japan had already captured the Philippines, Siam, Malaya, Singapore, Burma, the Dutch East Indies, Wake Island, the Gilbert Islands, New Britain, and Guam. The Allied forces were now ready to take on Admiral Yamamoto's Navy/Army forces.

Only three months earlier Japan had begun occupying Guadalcanal with 2,800 personnel (2,200 of which were Korean laborers), and Tulagi with 900 troops, to construct a forward base protecting its major base at Rabaul.

Former Pagota "Tower" of Japanese Honiara Airport, Guadalcanal,
October 6, 1942

Measuring eighty miles long and twenty-five miles wide, the island terrain was rugged with mountains soaring 8,000 feet high, making the Canal the second largest island in the Solomon Island chain. More importantly, when the large airfield being constructed at Lunga Point was completed, Japan's long range bombers would be able to attack any ships or forces operating in the sea lanes from the west coast of North America to the east coast of Australia. The Lunga Point airfield was the United States' primary objective during the invasion of the island. Taking out the planes and airfield prevented the Japanese fighters from defending the island. Further, it would be the jumping off point to attack Fiji, New Caledonia, Samoa, Australia, and New Zealand, moving Japan ever closer to positions from which it could attack the United States. In all, when the airfield was completed, over forty fighters and sixty bombers operated off Guadalcanal. The two islands needed to be taken, allowing the Allied forces to use them to advance our attack on mainland Japan.

The greatest carrier war in history began August 7, 1942, when the United States assembled an eighty-ship invasion force—including forces from Australia, New Zealand, and the United Kingdom—to attack the Japanese stronghold Guadalcanal. Three carriers, the *Enterprise, Saratoga*, and *Wasp* were at the center of the task force ready to provide air cover for the initial landing. Walter's *Portland* was in the battle group supporting the *Wasp*.

Sixteen thousand Marines were about to land on the beaches in the forever-remembered Higgins boats, the design of which was stolen from the Japanese. This time they were on the receiving end of these magnificent troop-and-equipment landing craft. The Japanese watched as the Marines swung over the sides of the troop ships four and five abreast, climbing down the rope landing nets hanging over the sides of the ships into the Higgins boats. The Marines had practiced going down and back up the nets as quickly as possible, many times, in preparation for this landing. The Japanese could easily identify the Marines wearing their green herringbone twill dungarees, helmets, packs with shelter halves rolled and tied on top, cartridge belts around their waists, leggings around their calves, boondocks, and rifles slung over their shoulders. These were America's elite landing troops, coming to attack and kill as many Japanese soldiers as they could find, who were often hidden in caves and hillside machine gun nests. The loaded Higgins boats circled near the transports until all were loaded. Japanese artillery were firing at the ships and the Higgins boats, even small arms rounds were fired into the boats in an effort to kill the Marines before they reached shore. With the boats bobbing in the choppy waters—caused by all the ships and boats in the water, shells landing in the water, and attacks by Japanese fighters—the Marines were more than ready to hear the command "Away All Boats." Though naval artillery had been pounding the island for some time, it could not be taken from the air. The only way the island could be taken was with Marine *boots on the ground*. As bullets and shells flew overhead, fighter planes engaged in dogfights, some crashing into the water around the Higgins boats—but the Marines had to wait for the ramp door to come down when they neared the beach. As they ran off the ramp, they plunged into water, sometimes up to their chests, as they moved onto the beach under an increasing hail of fire. Flopping down in the sand, they returned fire into the jungle from which they were being fired upon. *"Move out as quickly as you can,"* were the orders being hollered by their fire team, squad, and platoon leaders. Once the Marines reached the beach, the fighting grew intense. They had to fight their way off the beach and into the jungle, while buddies were being killed all around them. Those who were pinned down pulled out their entrenching tools and quickly dug holes in the sand, lowering their silhouette until they could again advance. Getting into the cover of the jungle was their goal, but some never made it, dying on the beach. When there were obstacles or mine fields in their path, Bangalore torpedo tubes were pushed ahead and detonated, clearing a safe path within which the Marines could advance. By day two, the Marines had taken Lunga Point.

NAVAJO CODE TALKERS

Accompanying the Marines were their newest secret weapons, Navajo code talkers. Philip Johnson, son of a missionary, had lived and worked with Navajo Indians near Flagstaff, Arizona, since 1896. He had also served as a Navajo/English translator between Navajo leaders and President Theodore Roosevelt. In May 1942, Johnson recognized the Japanese had translators in the Pacific who could listen to the Marines in battle and know, in advance, how and where the Marines would attack. Johnson had an idea how he could help, and proposed the Marine Corps use Navajos to communicate with the Marine commanders on the islands. Neither the Japanese nor anyone else could speak or understand the language. The Corps immediately liked the idea, and recruited the first 200 Navajo into the Marine Corps at Fort Defiance, Arizona, on May 4, 1942.

After completion of boot camp and language training at the Marine Recruit Depot in San Diego, the Navajo recruits moved to Camp Pendleton, where all the Marines trained prior to departing for the Pacific. The first thirteen Navajo code talkers landed with the Marines near Lunga Point, just four months later, on September 18. Until then, knowing the Japanese were listening to the Marine radio conversations, radiomen had to use code sheets to transmit coded messages. Messages were then decoded on the receiving end, all of which took valuable time in combat conditions, where seconds meant the difference between life and death. But this time the Navajos just spoke to each other and the messages were conveyed to the Marines almost instantly. The immediate advantages for the Marines were fewer lives lost, and they were able to advance their positions far more rapidly than before. Later, in the Battle of Iwo Jima, Major Howard Connor, signal officer for the 5th Marine Division said, "Were it not for the Navajos, we Marines would never have taken Iwo Jima."

The Navajo code talkers continued to be an incredible secret asset to the Corps until the end of the war. The Navajo code talkers program was not declassified until 1968. In December 2000, President Clinton awarded the Congressional Gold Medal to the Navajo code talkers, of which four survivors were present. A monument to the Navajo code talkers is located far out in the desert on the grounds of the Window Rock Navajo Tribal Park and Veteran's Memorial in northeast Arizona. The town Window Rock is the seat and capital of the sovereign Navajo nation, and largest of all the Native American nations. What is particularly notable is the park was not built by our federal government. It was designed and built solely by the Navajo.

As the battle for control of the island raged on, utilization of the airfield was a top priority task assigned to the Seabee's 6th Construction Battalion. The first Seabee's from companies A and D arrived September 1, just twenty-four days after the Marines landed. The 3,800-foot-long, 150-foot-wide runway was full of bomb craters that needed to be filled. Then the strip was lengthened 1,300 feet, cleared, and graded before a metal flexible Marston mat was laid so American planes could be brought in. The Seabees often worked around the clock even while the Japanese continued to bomb and shell the airfield. Oftentimes the Seabees would work on one end of the field, while Marines engaged in fighting the Japanese at the other end. As soon as parts of the field were damaged, the Seabees set about repairing them. As the battle continued to rage, the airfield continued to be repaired and rebuilt, until the remaining Japanese forces left the island, ending the battle in February 1943.

On that first day, an islander named Jacob Charles Vouza, born on Guadalcanal and retired less than one year earlier from the Solomon Islands Protectorate Armed Constabulary, was about to show where his loyalties lay. Having returned to active duty when the Japanese invaded the island, he was serving as a coast watcher. Sighting one of the pilots from the *Wasp* being shot down, Vouza rescued and guided the pilot to friendly lines. Later that month, while scouting for the 1st Marine Division, he was captured by the Japanese, tied to a tree, bayoneted in his arms, throat, shoulder, face, and stomach while being questioned about locations of the Marine forces. Vouza didn't talk and was left to die, tied to the tree. A short time later he managed to untie himself and walked several miles to the American Marine lines, giving them valuable information about the Japanese forces before he was hospitalized and his wounds treated. A short twelve days later he was assigned to Marine Lieutenant Colonel Evans Carlson's 2nd Marine Raider Battalion when they made their famous thirty-day raid behind Japanese lines to defend Henderson Field. It became known as "Edson's Bloody Ridge." Vouza received a Silver Star and Legion of Merit for his actions by 1st Marine Division commander Major General Alexander A. Vandegrift, and the British George Medal for gallant conduct. Later he would receive the Police Long Service Medal, and in 1957 he was made a member of the British Empire. In 1979, he was knighted by Queen Elizabeth II during her visit to the islands. Sergeant Major Vouza died in 1984, a loyal friend and comrade to the U.S. Marines, and a WWII combat war hero.

For some of the Marines in Fox Company, 2nd Battalion, 26th Marine Regiment, 5th Marine Division, their war ended on the beaches or the edge of the jungle on Guadalcanal, including one of their Navy Corpsman, Petty Officer 2nd Class Ed McHenry. Only two weeks after landing and moving into the jungle, Ed was stopping the bleeding, protecting the wounds, and preventing shock as fast as he could. His Marine buddies were being hit all around him. Caring for one Marine with a bad gut wound, Ed rose in a half crouch and ran forward toward another Marine who had just hollered *"Corpsman,"* when he was hit in the lower torso and went down. Unable to get to his feet, Ed was evacuated to Guam for treatment, eventually being sent all the way back to Hawaii to recuperate. His recovery would take a long time. No matter how much he wanted and asked to be returned to his unit, Ed's war was over.

Late in October, a Marine legend was made. "Manila" John Basilone had the background typical of a Marine. Born in New York, the son of an Italian immigrant, Basilone was raised in New Jersey. In 1934, at the age of eighteen, he joined the Army and saw duty in the Philippines until he was discharged in 1937. While working as a truck driver in Maryland, John, like

Walter Beckham, knew war was coming. Also like Walter, John wanted to be a part of it. Reasoning he would see fighting sooner as a Marine than re-enlisting in the Army, he joined the Marines in 1940. He was first sent to U.S. Naval Base, Guantanamo Bay, Cuba, before hitting the beach on Guadalcanal. Sergeant Basilone was leading two sections of heavy machine guns defending Henderson Field from Lunga Ridge, above the airfield, when a Japanese Sendai regiment attacked. Though the water-cooled machine guns were capable of firing continuously until freezing up under the intense heat, John ordered his gunners to keep firing as the Japanese bodies piled up in front of them. When two of his men were killed and three wounded, the Japanese broke through the defense line. John grabbed one of the machine guns jammed with mud, cleared the jam, and sprayed frantically into the rushing Japanese who were throwing grenades and mortar fire at the Americans. One Marine buddy said he could see the bayonets glistening on the Japanese rifles as they fired at John. For a while the attack was halted. Early the next morning, in a last ditch Bonsai charge, the Japanese came again. With only two of his men able to carry on, and while under continuous fire, John placed one gun in action, quickly repaired another gun, and manned it himself, gallantly repelling the onslaught while waiting anxiously for replacements to arrive. With ammunition critically low and cut off from supply lines, Sergeant Basilone, armed with only a .45 pistol, fought through enemy lines obtaining shells for himself and his gunners. When the fighting ended for John, he was credited with killing thirty-eight Japanese in one of the most ferocious battles on Guadalcanal. Sergeant John Basilone would receive the Medal of Honor for his actions on Guadalcanal. Unfortunately, he died while fighting on the first day of the Battle of Iwo Jima in 1945.

Here is How Walter Recalled the Battle of Guadalcanal...

"Soon we were in the center of a tremendous convoy with ships of every description. There were carriers, cruisers, and destroyers in numbers larger than I had ever before seen on a single operation, and it seemed the cargo

ships and transports were all over everywhere. We knew then we were getting ready to attack one of the Japanese outposts, for it could only be for the purpose of attack that such a convoy would be prepared. This tremendous force began to form into a gigantic formation which spread over several square miles of the sea. The entire force was ringed by destroyers, and planes were patrolling all around us to prevent any submarine attacks. It was a beautiful and inspiring sight to look on every side and see ships as far as the eye could reach into the horizon. The long high outlines of the carriers stood out over all the rest and in comparison with the destroyers, they appeared gigantic. There were two ships with whose silhouettes some of us were not familiar, and we were told by some of the older men that these were Australian cruisers, probably the heavy cruiser HMAS Canberra (D33) and another.

Our course now became more westerly. Several days later, we stood off while the Marines did some practice landings on a group of friendly islands. After this practice for two or three days we began to proceed north. It was announced to us that we were bound for the Solomon Islands where we would attack the Japanese. We made our ships ready for battle, and the nervous tension, which always precedes an operation, began to manifest itself again.

On the morning of August 7, 1942, we were roused around 0300, and after a light breakfast, went to General Quarters stations where we expected to remain all that day, at the very least. During the interim between the Battle of Midway and this attack, I had succeeded in obtaining for myself another battle station which was more to my liking. I had become the assistant to the navigator on the ship and was to act as an official observer of any actions which we might have and take notes as the action occurred. This material was later to be used in writing the ship's log. This gave me an opportunity to be on the bridge whenever an action seemed to be likely, and during the action, so that I could hear all the information which was sent to the bridge and could also observe everything that happened so that I could take good notes. What I didn't realize at the time was, next to our AA guns, the bridge was the number one target of any Japanese fighters attacking us.

On this morning, I stood on deck and watched our carriers launch their attack groups well before daybreak. We were attached to a carrier task force, though some of the other cruisers and destroyers had gone with the transports and cargo ships to cover the actual landing. The planes were to go into attack just at daybreak and the transports and cargo ships would move in behind that attack and the shelling of the cruisers and destroyers which were covering them. The planes had their running lights on as they were launched, since it was still quite dark. One of them exploded shortly after it was launched when something went wrong, and the explosion produced a bright red light momentarily before it died out. The rest of the planes began circling the formation and getting into their assigned positions. The roar of the motors was very loud and from our bridge, we could see several carriers launching their planes at the same time. It was a magnificent sight. As soon as all of the planes had been launched, it looked almost as if the sky was filled with fireflies since the red and green lights of the planes seemed to be everywhere. Finally the last circle was completed and they swung away to attack the Japanese. Our job was now one of watchful waiting and it is a nerve-rending job. The aviators were to open up on their radios when they got over the targets and until that time, we would not know what was happening unless we were attacked by the Japanese. The islands which we were attacking were Guadalcanal and Tulagi, where the main Japanese forces in the vicinity were centered. Shortly after daybreak, we heard our first pilots talking over the targets and it was only through their conversations, which we could hear on our receivers that we could understand what was going on. We could overhear the squadron leaders giving bombing and strafing commands to their pilots in support of the ground forces. We knew then our transports had arrived and were unloading the Marines on the beach and that they were encountering some resistance, though we could not tell how much. We heard one of the pilots tell another to go down and strafe a causeway since our troops seemed to be having difficulty getting across it. We later learned it was the causeway leading from Florida Island to the Island of Tanambogo where our casualties were heavy, since the Japs were dug in on Tanambogo with a series of well-constructed pill boxes and other fortifications. Another pilot yelled he was going down to blast a Japanese supply depot.

As soon as the pilots had exhausted their supply of bombs, they returned to the carriers and were reloaded, then took off again and returned to battle. All day long, in what seemed to be an incredibly long day, this shuttle bombing continued and all of the action that we could see were our planes returning to get new loads of explosives. We could see Guadalcanal on the horizon as it loomed up before us and seemed to be a mountainous place. All we could see, however, was its outline, though once we got close enough to see some gun flashes. We could not tell how the battle was progressing except we knew we had definite air superiority since we had not been attacked by planes ourselves. We were later to learn our aviators had taken the Japanese so completely by surprise that some twelve of their flying boats had been caught on the water and destroyed before they had a chance to get into the air. We also later were to learn of the great success of the Marines in their landings, though they suffered casualties on Tanambogo, Gavutu, and Tulagi Islands where the Japanese had established some fortifications and were not taken so completely by surprise.

That night we were a bit jittery since things seemed to be running almost too smoothly. We were cruising some distance away from Guadalcanal, however, and thus did not see any of the action which took place in that area. During the next day, we sent additional planes out for bombing raids and continued to cruise some distance removed from the islands. That night we were not aware of the battle which raged around Savo Island and in which three of our cruisers, the Quincy, Vincennes, Astoria and the Australian cruisers, the Canberra, were sunk. The heat lightning, which is prevalent in that area, gave some of us some bad moments as it greatly resembles the flashes of guns over the horizon.

Our particular task force remained in the area for some time after the initial attack. We patrolled the area and our assumption was we were being held in readiness to beat off any possible Japanese counter attack in an attempt to recapture parts or all of the islands we now occupied. After the first several days past without action, we began to relax since it appeared the Japanese had been caught unprepared and were not yet ready to launch a counterattack. In this, however, we were sorely mistaken.

The Japs were concentrating their forces in the Rabaul area north of Guadalcanal and were bombing our positions on Guadalcanal every day. At night they sent in surface ships to bombard our Marine positions on the island. However, they had not yet been able to bring up reinforcements for their troops. Unknown to most of us, on the morning of August 23rd, a group of Japanese transports had been sighted north of Guadalcanal. We, along with another carrier task force, were just out of sight over the horizon and southeast of Guadalcanal. During the night we moved north, and continued to protect allied communication lines.

On August 24 we were steaming not far distant from Stewart Island. Things had been very quiet and we had become so accustomed to our position of relative safety we no longer anticipated being attacked. As far as most of us knew, we hadn't even been spotted by the Japanese, nor had we seen any of their ships or planes. These days of patrol are the most trying and monotonous days of inactivity, compared to being engaged with the enemy. Watches continue to be stood in their regular routine and the ship's work progresses as usual. One day is the same as the next, and it was easy to forget which day of the week it was.

On this particular day it was bright and clear. The water was a pretty deep blue and calm. The ship's bow sent small ripples on either side as it cut cleanly through the water. At noon, we officers had our regular meal in the wardroom with the usual joviality and good-natured bantering back and forth between us. In the early afternoon, however, a single Jap observation plane was spotted as it streaked across a background of white puffy cumulous clouds. The plane almost circled our force before it was suddenly shot down by one of our fighters. Hearing it had been spotted, I rushed up on deck just in time to see the smoke rising from the burning oil where the plane had crashed into the sea. We knew it must have given our location back to the ship it flew off of. By mid afternoon a long blast of the Bo'sun's pipe over the loud speakers was the prelude to the call to General Quarters and all hands immediately went to their battle stations. I quickly went to the bridge, having first donned my flash proof clothing and helmet. When I arrived, there was some tension in the faces of our captain and the other officers present. I learned we were receiving reports of a large force of enemy planes heading our way, and at not too great a distance. In line with my duties as assistant to the navigator, I began jotting down notes of the various reports as they came into us. It was not long before it was apparent the Japanese were going to attack our battle group.

Our carrier had already launched its defensive squadron of fighter planes, and on the radio, we could hear them being directed to intercept the enemy who was coming in at us from a very high altitude. It was only a matter of several minutes before gunfire from the carrier was followed by fire from the other ships. The attack was under way. Within seconds some forty to fifty Japanese dive-bombers appeared, protected by a group of fighters, diving down on us from about ten thousand feet. Dogfights between our fighters and theirs quickly developed, and we shot down some fifteen to twenty before they started firing on us. The carrier was their only initial target, as it seems they picked our ship as a guide to when they would start their diving attack on our carrier. This was the first dive-bombing attack I had ever seen and I was more excited than anything else as I jotted down my notes of the action in progress. It was the first time I truly felt death imminent, and surviving would truly be a miracle.

The carrier appeared like some wild beast as she lunged and turned and veered attempting to shake off the bombers. It seemed to me they would never quit coming as I watched one after another peel off and dive down attacking our carrier. Our guns were blazing away fiercely and I gave credit to the anti-aircraft battery situated just below me for one of the planes shot down. In all, I saw some eight to ten more planes shot down as some lay burning on the surface of the ocean before they would sink below out of sight. Others were shot down that I couldn't see from my vantage point. At times it was questionable as to which fighters were ours and which were theirs as they came in and out of view, guns blazing as bullets and shells flew everywhere, and smoke filled the sky.

For the first time, I saw a plane diving at well over 300 miles an hour, failing to pull out of its dive, and plunging headlong into the sea, making but a small splash before disappearing from sight, somewhat like a swimmer executing a high dive hitting the water smoothly with little splash. I saw several bombs strike the carrier on her flight deck. One started a fire which was soon extinguished. The sky grew darker from the smoke of the guns and exploding shells. Our own ship had been turning violently, following the motions of the carrier in order to stay as close as possible and give the maximum protection we could.

One of the battle ships with our force had dropped a little behind the rest of the formation and several of the bombers singled her out for their attack. We later heard she destroyed all the planes which had attacked her, and sustained no damage. The attack actually lasted only a matter of a few minutes, but it seemed much longer as one after another the Jap planes came at us dropping their bombs and torpedoes, which could be followed on their course by our naked eyes. At times the carrier was almost completely obscured from sight by the waterspouts from near misses and smoke from explosions, and the spray resulting from her own maneuvers as she tried to escape the rain of bombs and torpedoes. Most of them did miss her, but several found their mark and after the attack, she was in a condition which called for repairs before she could again see action.

The carrier planes from our other task force, which had not been attacked, had in turn attacked the Japanese force. We later found that they had bombed a carrier and damaged a cruiser and a destroyer. Our carrier had been our only casualty with fairly severe damage. She was having difficulty in recovering her planes as part of her flight deck had been lifted by the explosion of a bomb, causing a hump on her deck just where the planes would normally touch down to be grabbed by the arresting gear. Toward dusk, I saw one of the fighters crash into the barrier on the carrier deck. No fire started, but the damaged plane had to be taken below.

We had a gorgeous tropical sunset which struck me with its irony – having seen death, violence and destruction in the afternoon. Come dusk, the carrier temporarily lost steering and our hearts sank. She slowed down to almost a dead stop and we began to circle around her. Visions of Midway began to come before me and the fate of the Yorktown. However, in a short time, the necessary repairs were made and we again got underway—much to our relief. The relief was short-lived, however, as a brilliant full moon arose out of the ocean. There was not a cloud in the sky and it looked almost as bright as day—at a time when we would have liked nothing better than to be plunged into utter darkness to avoid being seen. We knew full well the Japs knew our position, and we fully expected to see their torpedo planes again. The night passed, however, and no Japs ever materialized."

CHAPTER 6

WHERE ARE THEY?

The war in the Pacific was oftentimes a bit of a cat-and-mouse game. Using sonar, radio, code breakers, scout/observation planes, and intelligence reports, the Japanese Navy was looking for the American Navy, and the American Navy was looking for the Japanese Navy to engage in battle. The exceptions to these tactics were invasions of known land sites, such as the many islands located in the Pacific Ocean.

In August 1942, the *Portland* was engaged in a decisive battle of the Eastern Solomon Islands before steaming south to again provide carrier screening for the *Enterprise* at the Battle of Santa Cruz. Walter and his crew were now involved in combat more than not as they zigzagged back to the Solomons to help thwart the third attempt by the Japanese to retake Guadalcanal at the Battle of Savo Island. The Japanese had at least two battleships and several cruisers and destroyers in the waters around the island. The Americans, in addition to the *Enterprise*, had four cruisers—the *San Francisco, Helena, Juneau,* and *Atlanta,* along with several destroyers. General Quarters was once again the order of the day. The *Portland* and her crew were about to earn more campaign medals and service ribbons. Sometime during this period of time, Walter was promoted to lieutenant, Junior Grade (JG), effective October 1, 1942.

"SWEET PEA" IS HIT

Early in the morning of November 13, the *Portland* took a direct torpedo hit on her starboard side. The hit blew off the inboard propellers, causing the rudder to jam at five degrees right, as well as jamming the number three turret, and other damage yet to be identified. "Sweet Pea" took a four-degree starboard list as some of the crew started wondering if they would hear the order to abandon ship. Though the list was corrected by shifting fuel and water, "Sweet Pea" could only steam in circles to the right. She could not sail in any direction away from where she had been hit. She had been hit hard, but didn't hit the canvas. The *Portland* was just beginning to fight.

Finishing her first circle and illuminated by nearby burning ships and flares, her forward turrets opened fire on a Japanese battleship, which immediately fired salvos back at the *Portland*. Fortunately, the salvos all passed overhead, never hitting "Sweet Pea." This time she fired four, six-gun salvos that hit the battleship, starting several fires on the dreadnaught. Continuing to circle, several hours later she opened fire again with six-gun salvos on a Japanese destroyer from a range of 12,500 yards. The sixth salvo killed the destroyer as she exploded, rolled over, and sank within minutes. If the *Portland* was going to go down, her ship's Captain DuBose was going to make sure she took some Japanese with her.

The following morning, with several Higgins boats shoving on her starboard bow, the *Portland* began making slow progress to the southeast. Early afternoon saw a yard patrol boat (YP) come out to try and tow "Sweet Pea" in the right direction, without success. Finally, a tug came out from Tulagi, and towed her clear of the Solomons, where some adjustments were made, allowing the *Portland* to steer straight ahead instead of in circles. She then proceeded under her own power to Sydney, Australia, where additional repairs were made. Repairs were also made on the bodies and souls of her crew.

Many years later, Walter told Walter III that R&R in Sydney was well deserved and a most enjoyable relief from the stress of combat. He and a couple of other officers rented a flat in Kings Cross, and rotated their weekly stays there. Walter was invited to Thanksgiving dinner by a family that had befriended him. They even let him borrow their car. He was a young twenty-two year old, far away from home, who sorely missed the security and comfort of his own family and girlfriend. The Australians were very friendly to the Americans, as the Americans had kept the Japanese from attacking Australia. It took a bit of listening to understand the strong accent, but the pretty and friendly girls of the famous Kings Cross nightlife helped a lot in that regard. There were many parties in the bars and restaurants, and Walter, along with the rest of his crew, more than once woke up with a headache reminder of the revelry the night before.

Once repairs were completed, there were short stops at Samoa and Pearl Harbor before the ship reached Mare Island Navy Yard in San Francisco, on March 3, 1943, for a complete overhaul.

Walter Tells the Story...

"On the morning of November 8th, we weighed anchor and began to get underway for waters yet unknown to the crew. As we proceeded out of the harbor, we passed the gallant Enterprise with whom we had shared so much of battle and anxiety. Attention on deck was sounded and all hands stood at attention facing the Enterprise as we came abreast and passed her. She returned our salute and it was with a tinge of reluctance I saw we were leaving her behind. Quickly passing the other ships, we then made our way through the tortuous reefs which surrounded the mouth of the anchorage at Noumea, New Caledonia.

Joined by other ships, including the light anti-aircraft cruiser USS Juneau (CL-52), some four or five destroyers and mine sweepers, and seven or eight transports, our mission was to convoy these ships to Guadalcanal where they would unload their troops and supplies to reinforce our weary Marines. Our course having been set, we settled down quickly to the routine of again being underway.

On November 10, the U.S. Marine Corps birthday, we rendezvoused with another force which consisted of the heavy cruiser USS San Francisco (CA-38), and the light cruisers USS Helena (CL-50) and USS Atlanta (CL-51), and four or five destroyers. The next day we approached the southern region of the Solomon Islands. It was a far cry from the Armistice days which we had known back home; but the weather was good and our spirits were high. In the afternoon the transports, with a small destroyer escort, dropped astern of the rest of our group. The plan was the cruisers and destroyers would go into Sea Lark Channel between Guadalcanal and Florida Island, and proceed to the northern entrance to the channel around Savo Island, for an all-night patrol. We were to contact and destroy any enemy ships we found in those waters, to insure our transports would encounter no opposition when they came in to off load at dawn on the 12ᵗʰ.

We went to General Quarters just after the evening meal and remained at our battle stations all night. I shall never forget the ghostly experience of that night. It was a very dark night with no moon, and we entered a narrow channel after darkness had thoroughly set in. Our heavy ships, which consisted of the two heavy and three light cruisers, were in a battle-line, flanked by the destroyers. Everything was completely blacked out and our speed had been greatly reduced. From my position on the bridge, I could see a long, dark outline of Guadalcanal off our port side. The breeze brought out the lush, dank, tropical sweet smell which only the island jungles can produce. It reminded me of the sweetish smell of night-blooming jasmine during summer time in the South. At intervals, we could see small navigation lights which, according to pre-arranged plans, flicked on from time to time, in order that we might get our bearings and not bump into something. The night air was cool and refreshing. I noticed a subdued light off our port side in the jungle and was told it was the light from Henderson Field on Guadalcanal. It died out at intervals and then would reappear. It evidently was allowing planes to take off or land.

As we proceeded farther into the channel, I could see the barrels from a Japanese gun position which was firing toward our positions around the airfield. It appeared to be of approximately five-inch caliber and it was pouring a steady stream of shells at our Marines. The night remained very quiet, other than this, and we arrived at the northern entrance to the channel without making any contact whatsoever. I could see the outline of Savo Island as it loomed ahead of us and my thoughts were of the cruisers which we had lost there in early August. We swung to starboard, remaining in formation, and headed toward Florida Island to begin our all-night vigil.

Motor torpedo boats from our base at Tulagi had been sent out beyond us to the north to also patrol. They had been instructed, however, not to attack any ships they might contact – but to allow them to pass through until our force could make contact with them. Upon approaching Florida Island, we circled and reversed course, going again toward Savo Island and Guadalcanal, in order to preserve our grip on the entrance to the channel. The night wore on very quietly and slowly. All of us were under some tension as we fully expected we might make contact with some part of the famed "Tokyo Express" which had been steadily reinforcing and resupplying the Japanese forces in the Northern Solomons. It usually consisted of fast light cruisers and destroyers. The night, however, passed without contact.

At dawn on the morning of the 12th, we proceeded south toward Lunga Point as the transports approached from the south. It was here the unloading was to take place. The channel was calm and the dawn was beautiful as we looked toward the mountain range which ran along the Guadalcanal shoreline. There was beach before the jungle began, and then it went uphill. How the Marines triumphed there is beyond comprehension. It looked almost like an early morning scene in the Blue Ridge Mountains of the southeastern United States. Still in the battle-line as we approached Lunga Point, our lead destroyer had submarine contact and began to fire into the water off its stern, with a five-inch gun. All our ships began to scatter and pick up speed. The contact was soon lost, however, and our ships again approached the Point. Transports came as close to the shore as possible and at once began off loading into the fleets of Higgins boats which had been sent out from the beach, while the cruisers patrolled in a leisurely semi-circle off shore, and the destroyers provided submarine protection.

As we approached within several hundred yards of the beach we could plainly see the Marines on shore. We could see jeeps driving on roads along the shore and also pitched camouflage tents in the coconut grove immediately up from the beach. With the Japanese troops temporarily pulled back, some of the Marines were washing clothes and swimming in the water. This was quite a treat, and great relief for the Marines, as we had never been this close to frontline action on the ground.

The unloading continued unabated throughout the morning. In mid-morning, "Pistol Pete," a Jap gun trained on the harbor and landing area, fired a shell which landed in the center of our ships formation. The admiral detached the Helena and two destroyers to move up the beach and silence the gun. Assisted by an observation spotter plane, "Pistol Pete" was silenced. The Helena and the destroyers also found a large group of Japanese landing boats and sank many of them before they set large piles of supplies aflame. It was a beautiful sight to watch the rapid fire of the Helena as she sent salvo after salvo from her six and five-inch guns into the Japanese positions. We also watched some of our Dauntless dive-bombers as they dove down and attacked other Japanese sites. The Marines on the beaches just opposite continued to excite our curiosity as the unloading continued.

Around fifteen hundred, we were notified by Henderson Field, that a large group of enemy torpedo-planes were headed in our direction. Immediately the air-raid sirens whined on all our ships as a warning to prepare to repel the air attack. The transports and cargo ships began to get under way, surrounded by the cruisers and destroyers. Our force moved away from the shore toward the channel center in order that we might have as much room as possible in which to maneuver during the attack. We did not have to wait long.

Approximately twenty Japanese torpedo-planes of the large two-engine type with fighter cover by some ten Zeros began to make their approach from the south. The enemy had gone around our positions and come at us from the direction of Florida Island; in this way, attempting to elude our fighter squadrons which had been sent up from Henderson Field to intercept them. Normally the Japanese attacked coming in from the north. This ruse was not entirely successful, however, and out beyond the reach of our anti-aircraft barrage, we were able to see dog fights between our fighters and the Zeros, and also some of the torpedo planes falling from the sky with long trails of smoke streaming from them. Torpedo planes came in at a very low altitude—and when they came within range of our ships' guns, we unleashed a terrific barrage of anti-aircraft fire. The barrage became so hot and heavy that one of the Japanese planes, which I saw drop its torpedo several thousand yards away, swerved to attempt an escape over Florida Island. I then saw the most spectacular kill by one of our fighter planes I had ever witnessed. This Grumman "Cat" had been standing off at about 3,000 feet, out of our line of fire following the Japs and watching for a chance to swoop down when there was no danger of being hit by our own gunfire. When he saw this torpedo plane turn away, he made one long dive directly for it and I could see the Japanese tail gunner in the torpedo plane firing at the Grumman as he came down. The Grumman paid no heed, and when he was within range, he raked the bomber from one end to the other with machine gun fire before pulling gradually out of his dive. The torpedo bomber began to wobble and in a matter of seconds, it was smoking. A few seconds later, it went completely out of control crashing into the sea, leaving only a spot of burning oil on the surface of the water to mark the place where it fell.

The rest of the Japanese planes continued toward our force but the anti-aircraft fire was so severe that at one time, I saw two Jap fighters fall into the sea at the same time. One of the planes had been set afire attempting to do a Bonsai crash into the San Francisco. When Japanese fighter/bombers have fired all their bombs, they would often attempt to crash their planes into an American ship as a last honorable act of suicide called Bonsai. In this it was only partially successful as the right wing tip caught a director in the aft part of the ship, and as the wing sheared off, it filled the director with fire. The main part of the plane was carried forward by its momentum beyond the ship and crashed into the water near the stern of the destroyer.

The torpedo attack was a total failure, as none of our ships took a direct hit, and out of the approximate thirty planes involved in the attack, we heard only one escaped. Our protecting fighters and gunfire had accounted for the rest.

I had caught one glimpse of the Marines on the shore during the attack, and although there was no effective way in which they could assist us, I shall never forget the feeling of surprise which I experienced when I saw some of them continuing to wash their clothes and walk along the beach, seemingly as if nothing out of the ordinary was happening.

After the attack was over, the transport and cargo ships returned to their unloading points where they were again met by the Higgins boats, and resumed unloading. The Japs didn't bother us for the rest of the afternoon. I spent the rest of the day watching the Marines in their small craft removing the debris and some bodies from the spots where the Jap planes had fallen. We were very envious of this opportunity to get souvenirs of battle, as we had not before been this close to the spoils. Previously we had always left the scene of action as quickly as possible and were moving away even before the action stopped.

As the sun again began to set, and the unloading had been completed, we moved away from the Marines and started south as if we were leaving for good. Evidently the Japs believed this to be our plan, as they saw us depart. After we escorted the cargo and transport ships from the area and the dark of night fell on us, most of the fighting ships turned back, leaving one lone destroyer to escort the others away. We retraced our course and began to repeat our performance of the previous night. Again we steamed in ghostly silence up the dark channel and again we were at our battle stations. This being the second night at our battle stations, it was arranged some of the men could sleep on station in shifts. They remained near enough to their stations, however, so they could be called back at the first sign of danger. At my particular station in the coding room, we arranged to relieve each other with two man shifts throughout the night. Since my battle station was as an observer, and as there seemed no likelihood of battle to us, I spent the first part of the evening talking with the supply officer and peering out into the darkness. We considered this night was to be but a repetition of the previous one of silent patrol. Our thoughts were fairly light and our conversation likewise – though we were still under the tension of the afternoon air attack.

About 2200 that evening, I became unbearably sleepy and suggested to my shipmate I should like to take a nap. He agreed, and as my turn in the coding room was still several hours distant, I retired into the wardroom where I removed my helmet and shoes, laid down on a couch along the bulkhead and went fast asleep. We approached the sound off Lunga Point shortly after midnight. Unknown to most of us, though well known to our carrier admirals and ships captains, was that during the previous afternoon a large Japanese force had been sighted north of us. Coming into the sound in a single battle-line with four destroyers at the head, five cruisers in the center, and four destroyers in the rear, we ran squarely into that force which had divided into several groups. We were at very close range before either side opened fire as it was a very dark night. We tracked the Japs in, following them with our guns for several minutes before firing commenced. The precipitant action which started the battle occurred when a leading Japanese destroyer turned on its search light and slowly turned it around until it pointed squarely on our ships. We opened fire.

Our first salvo woke me with a start. I jumped from the couch and trembling with excitement, began to put on my helmet and shoes. I saw the supply officer jump out of the chair where he had been napping, plop on his helmet and head for the open deck outside the wardroom. I was right behind him, but I took the passageway outside the officers' galley and found three of our mess attendants gathered there. One of them had a broad grin on his face which struck me as being very odd. Beyond them I met one of the most colorful characters on our ship. An ensign, having been promoted from the enlisted ranks, he had some twenty odd years in the Navy and had, at one time, been a contender for Navy heavy-weight boxing champion honors. He always smoked a cigar and packed a .45 cal pistol on his hip, which was a relic of the days when he had been Chief Master at Arms of the ship. I asked him what was going on and he said he didn't know, but that there was a damn good battle going on out there. I pushed aside the blackout canvas curtains and went out on deck. Not yet needing to be at my battle station, I saw a weird and awesome sight from amidships. The eerie green light from star shells and flares bursting illuminated the sky. I could see ships firing on all sides and the noise and concussion of our own guns was severe, making my head pound. We had sunk a Jap destroyer with our first salvo and had now switched to a second and larger target. I ran across the deck and taking an inboard ladder, climbed up one deck to the Foc'sle deck where I could get a better view of what was happening. From there I moved to the starboard side to see one of our light cruisers, astern of us, open fire. Her guns belched forth shells like a mighty battery of Roman candles on the Fourth of July. As I stood watching her, we were hit by a torpedo fired from a Japanese destroyer. It struck us some thirty to forty feet from our stern, causing a tremendous hole, jamming our rudder and knocking off two of our four screws, plus putting our number 3, eight-inch turret gun out of commission. Fortunately the hit didn't start any fires and did not explode the magazine in the turret. It seemed, as I looked, that the entire stern of our ship was being blown into the air and I made a dive for the center of the ship where I sat flat on the deck with my back against a bulkhead. Looking out toward the stern, I realized there was a group of other men around me and I was praying aloud.

Our two forward eight-inch turrets and our secondary batteries continued to fire after we had been hit, although we had lost steering control and were circling to the right. This forced us to drop out of our battle-line as our other ships continued to pass us and engage the enemy. Our inter-ship communication system had been put out of commission so we had no radio contact with our other ships. At one time a search light beam picked us out but then disappeared. Star shells continued to burst all around us. We were a sitting duck. I could see some of the large caliber shells from the Japanese ships as they passed over us like blazing balls of fire, ricocheting and bouncing along on top of the water until they hit something or their force was spent. One large shell hit us in our starboard hangar about fifty yards from where I was. It tore a big hole in the hangar, but caused little else damage. A repair crew stationed in the hangar escaped injury by following the battle-tested practice of lying flat on the deck when not actually engaged in repair work. We also suffered a small shell hit just below our starboard catapult just at the point where the armor plate on the side of the ship stopped, creating a small hole where we were taking on water until the repair crew plugged it. Large shells again passed over us with a roar like that of a rushing freight train, even louder than the noise from our secondary batteries firing. As I continued to look aft, I saw one of our destroyers with a raging fire on its stern, but with all guns forward firing and her searchlight beamed on an enemy destroyer, she was plunging headlong forward toward the enemy. A little fire wasn't going to hold her back.

It is impossible to describe the intensity of this action and the terrific force of its impact on one's psyche. The opposing forces had closed to ranges as low as from two to four thousand yards and with eight and fourteen-inch guns, it is almost impossible to miss one's target. We were duking it out until the last man fell. Having passed between two lines of enemy ships, the element of surprise had been in our favor, causing some of the enemy ships to actually fire on each other. It was also believed we had caught the Japanese ships with their guns and hoists filled with bombardment ammunition intended for use in blasting our shore installations and troops. Bombardment ammunition is set to explode upon impact and thus cause the greatest damage without penetrating deeply into the target. These shells were not intended for ship to ship targets, which put the Japs at a decided disadvantage. The prime object in naval warfare is for the projectile to penetrate the ship before exploding, thus causing additional internal explosions, even damaging machinery or blowing up magazines. In this battle, we scored a decided blow with our gunfire before the surprised Japs could switch their ammo.

The Portland had fired at three main targets. The first had been the destroyer which we sunk with our first salvo. Then we switched to a larger ship, possibly a cruiser, and put several salvos in her, as we watched her turn over. Sweet Pea, like her sister ship, would continue to fight even when seriously injured. Our third target, believed to be a battleship, received our remaining salvos. At this time we did not know the strength of the enemy force, but were certain it included one and possibly two battleships, several heavy and light cruisers, and accompanying destroyers. The damage to our force had been considerable, though we did not yet know the extent of the damage.

Finally, after what seemed a small eternity, but which was in reality only about thirty minutes, the firing ceased. There was still some sporadic gunfire, but it gradually died away. The quiet which followed was accompanied by a thick pall of oil smoke which permeated the entire area, thereby adding to the depressiveness of the scene. The smoke came from the burning ships and from ships which had burned before they sank. The opposing forces had met like two mighty waves which had thrown themselves against each other until one had finally smashed the force of the other – and all became quiet again. I got up from the deck and walked over to the side of the ship, being very thankful we were still afloat. The stink of the burning oil was very strong and though obscured by the smoke, I could see five ships burning on the horizon around us. We were roughly in the center of a circle in which they formed the perimeter. Our speed had been cut down until we were proceeding very slowly in a circle to the right. I stayed on the Foc'sle peering into the gloom with the others around me, including our chaplain and supply officer. Our wounded were being cared for in sick bay and our wardroom. There were others for whom no further care could be provided as they had given the supreme sacrifice of devotion to their country. The night seemed very long as we paced the deck. Our gun crews were still ready at their stations, prepared for any further action. Toward morning, one of the large ships which had been burning steadily through the night, suddenly blew up – her magazines exploded like another display of fire works. Finally she sank and we would later learn it was a Japanese cruiser. The other ships continued to burn, though it seemed that one of them was making some headway toward controlling her fires. We were to learn later this was our own gallant cruiser the Atlanta, which had sustained terrific damage while inflicting some mighty blows on the enemy. Two of the other three fires were our own destroyers, the USS Cushing (DD-376) and the USS Monssen (DD-436). Our destroyers suffered very heavily in this action. The fifth fire came from a Japanese destroyer.

When dawn came, we found we were several miles from shore between Lunga Point and Savo Island. The shore opposite us at Guadalcanal was still occupied by Japanese. We could see the Atlanta dead in the water with her whole bridge shot away, but with her fires under control. The water all around us was filled with debris and survivors who had been in the water for several hours. Two apparently dead Japs came floating by us on a piece of wreckage. We began to make preparations for picking up some of the survivors and put a life raft and motor whaleboat over the side to aid in the rescue. After the motor whaleboat cleared the ship and started picking up survivors, we turned our attention to a Japanese destroyer still burning from the night before. It was trying to get behind Savo Island, but was only able to make two or three knots of speed. I was told our captain asked them if they would surrender and their answer was to begin firing at us. We were well out of their range, however, and since we were just beginning to circle away from it, we waited until our arc brought us into firing position for our two forward eight-inch turrets and we then opened fire. Many of the crew who were not assigned to guns remained on deck since there was little else of benefit we could do. After the terrible shock of the night before, the noise and concussion of our guns firing again was even worse than usual. Our first salvo was short and to the left. Our second long and to the right, but with our third salvo we began to get a range. The fourth salvo straddled the Jap ship and produced a hit. Our fifth salvo hit the aft-magazines and the destroyer literally disappeared in a cloud of smoke. When the cloud rose from the water, the destroyer was not to be seen and a mighty cheer went up from our crew. Our nervous tension was at such a peak it had to have an outlet. The black cloud from the destroyer was of such proportion we could continue to see it as it ascended high into the sky, hovering over the spot where the enemy ship had been. I thought I could see what appeared to be a lifeboat out beyond the spot. At this time we could also see a cross piece on the foremast of a Japanese battleship on the horizon. The battleship had been damaged in the night action and had been left behind with a destroyer escort when the main body of the Japs pulled back. This filled us with apprehension, as we did not know the extent of the damage to the battleship, or whether it was returning to the scene to finish off any of our crippled ships remaining in the area. It began firing on the Aaron Ward, another of our destroyers which was dead in the water. However, planes from Henderson Field began arriving and took on the task of destroying the battleship. After receiving several torpedo hits from our bombers throughout the day, she continued on her course away from the action. Late that night she was last seen burning and was moving at less than five knots. On the morning of the 14th, it was nowhere to be found and presumed to have sunk during the night. In addition to the battleship, it is believed we sank several Japanese cruisers and destroyers. But most important, we had succeeded in turning back the advance striking force before they were able to inflict any damage to our troops ashore.

After the Japanese destroyer sank, our motor whaleboat returned to the ship filled with survivors and pulling two life rafts full of men behind it. Once on board the survivors needed attention. Many were wounded and they were all soaked with oil which was in their eyes, nose, mouth, ears, and some had even unintentionally swallowed it. Doctors and corpsmen ministered to them in the temporary sickbay set up in our wardroom. Sadly, one died after arriving on board. At this, a fleet of Higgins boats arrived from Lunga Point, so we hauled in our motor whaleboats and left the rest of the rescue work to the Higgins boats.

Our main job was now to attempt to save our ship. The Higgins boats came in among the survivors and began picking them out of the water. We heard later the Marines shot some of the Japanese who began to fire on them with pistols or who refused to be rescued. Concentrating our energies now on our attempt to retire from the battle scene and save our ship seemed almost hopeless. We could not make any headway going forward as we could only circle to the right like country square dancers. We felt like a duck after one wing had been wounded and it was only able to flounder in the pond, unable to fly. Word was sent to our headquarters at Guadalcanal for any assistance that could be given. It so happened there was one small tug and a YP boat in Tulagi Harbor that were sent to assist us. But when they arrived alongside the Portland, Captain Du Bose ordered the tug to tow the Atlanta to a position opposite Lunga Point first, as she was unable to move under her own power and had only a few of her guns able to fire. Plus, she had suffered heavier casualties than us.

In the meantime, the YP boat was to try and take us under tow. Unfortunately, the hole in our stern, combined with our jammed rudder exerted tremendous stress on the tow line that it broke loose twice. Finally, we began to make a little progress by backing down and steering with our engines. It was painstakingly slow as the morning dragged on, and we were constantly expecting to be attacked by Japanese planes or a submarine we were confident would be sent to finish us off. As time passed we spotted one of our protective cover planes begin to dive toward the water, strafing with her machine guns. We guessed it must be attacking an enemy sub, but nothing came of it. Later, Henderson Field reported planes were approaching from the north and our air-raid siren sounded though we were already at our battle stations. The enemy planes never reached us as our air cover took them out or turned them away. But the Japanese planes kept coming, yet not one made it through our air defense which had been thrown up around us. All morning we could see the black patches of anti-aircraft fire on the horizon which told us our planes were continuing to press home their attacks against the wounded Jap battleship and the cordon of destroyers attempting to protect it.

While watching the Marines in their Higgins boats continue to search for survivors of the night action, the tug, having safely towed the Atlanta, came back to help us. After several attempts to take us under tow had failed, she was brought alongside and lashed to our starboard side well forward of amidships. The YP was then lashed to her side, thus enabling both to push against our starboard side counteracting the tremendous pull by the rudder and hole. Four or five Higgins boats were even brought up placing their bows on our starboard side, and began pushing against us. Gradually they would slip forward and as each one was pushed past the bow of the ship, it would circle around and take its place again at the aft end of the line. With this arrangement we were able to make much better headway, though it was painstakingly slow. The strain of the previous thirty-six hours was becoming more and more apparent on all of the crew. All looked haggard and worn, and all were as nervous as a cat. The afternoon wore on and we were still several miles from Tulagi Harbor and well out in the channel. Every now and then it was necessary for us to stop completely while the tug and Higgins boats pushed our bow again in the proper direction, as we still had a tendency to go to the right. When dusk came, most of us wouldn't have given a plug nickel for our chances of coming through. With the coming of night and its poor visibility, which would remove the effectiveness of our air cover, we were certain the Japs would send some sort of an attack by ship or submarine to sink us. I was on the Bridge early that evening, when a Higgins boat was sent off our port side to investigate an object in the water. In a few minutes it returned reporting a submarine was, in deed, lying off our port side firing torpedoes at us. We never received any confirmation, and we were never hit, nor was any submarine ever sighted. The report only served to increase our tension. Some time later we saw a bright searchlight beam appear in the direction of Guadalcanal. The Japs were again looking for us. We watched breathlessly as the beam of light passed around us. On the return swing it did hesitate and then was suddenly turned off. We never knew its source.

The tug and YP boat were still struggling valiantly to help us limp into port. The YP, however, was showering sparks from her funnel and our captain sent a frantic message that it was a matter of life and death that the sparks be stopped, since they were a dead give-away as to our position. I shall never forget the answer from the YP skipper. In a voice almost in desperation, he sent back he didn't know what he could do as he already had two men stationed at the top of the funnel with a screen and salt-water hose spraying on the funnel trying to keep the sparks from escaping, but he would try. As if matters could not get worse, at about this time our radioman tuned in on the intership communications hearing a PT boat squadron based in Tulagi Harbor, had surrounded us with four or five of their boats and the commanders were discussing whether or not they should attack us with their torpedoes or guns. In the excitement of the day, they had not been notified we were proceeding into Tulagi Harbor. All they knew was there was a large ship approaching dangerously close to their base that might well be Japanese. We quickly went on the air and identified ourselves to their satisfaction. We then asked them to get us a pilot to guide us into the harbor, as it was now about 2130 and very dark. We continued our approach and shortly thereafter a pilot came aboard and brought us in to anchorage, though it was decided not to take us in very far that night, but to anchor us just behind a ridge overlooking the mouth of the harbor, thereby hiding us from view. When the anchor was let go the men went to sleep almost where they stood from sheer exhaustion and fatigue. As luck would have it, about a half hour later a powerful searchlight cut across the harbor's entrance not 500 yards away, but the cliff hid us from view. The light was from a Japanese cruiser which was later attacked by our PT boats as it joined several other ships shelling Henderson Field. The heavens were again lit up from the flashes of the guns. Even with all the noise from the guns, I lay down on the deck of the bridge, still in my steel helmet, life jacket and flash-proof jacket and got some of the best sleep I ever had. When I awoke several hours later the bridge was deserted except for lookouts. I went below and slept the rest of the night."

When the battle for Guadalcanal finally ended on February 9, 1943, the casualties on both sides were astronomical:

ALLIED FORCES	JAPANESE
7,100 killed	31,000 killed
4 captured	1,000 captured
29 ships lost	38 ships lost
615 aircraft lost	683-880 aircraft lost

For the Marines buried in a makeshift cemetery on Guadalcanal, an epitaph describes the greatest victory and heroic American offensive in the Pacific in WWII, which reads: *And when he gets to Heaven to Saint Peter he will tell "One more Marine reporting, Sir, I've served my time in Hell!"*

Mount Suribach, Iwo Jima

Among those Marines who landed on Iwo Jima and Saipan were members of the 51st Defense Battalion, the first all-black unit in the Marine Corps. When the battle for Iwo Jima was over, Admiral Nimitz memorialized the Marines who fought there saying "uncommon valor was a common virtue." The only other all-black unit in the Corps at the time, the 52nd Defense Battalion, served with distinction on Guam, Ellice Islands, and the Mariana Islands by war's end.

Black men had been serving in the Army and the Navy, but not the Marine Corps. It wasn't until Eleanor Roosevelt and Mary McLeod Bethune (black educator and civil rights activist) decided they could help the war effort in yet another way, by getting black men to be allowed to serve in the Corps. In 1936, President Roosevelt had appointed Mary Bethune director, Division of Negro Affairs of the National Youth Administration. And so it was that Eleanor Roosevelt and Mary Bethune caused President Roosevelt to sign into law Executive Order 8802 in June 1941, creating the Fair Employment Practices Commission, which banned racial discrimination in the defense industry. Howard Perry was the first black man to enlist in September 1942. Black Marines received boot camp training at Montford Point, a satellite camp of Camp Lejeune in North Carolina. The tall and powerful Edgar Huff became one of the first drill instructors at Montford Point, and went on to become the first black sergeant major. His brother-in-law, Master Sergeant Gilbert "Hashmark" Johnson, gained notoriety because he had more service stripes on his forearm sleeves than rank stripes on his bicep sleeves. "Hashmark" had served in the Army and then the Navy before finally being allowed to join the Marine Corps, which was his first choice. Soon after WWII, the Corps became fully integrated and the black units were disbanded. The Montford Point Marines had paved the way, showing their prowess in and out of combat, equal to that of any other Marine. 1949 saw the first black female, Annie N. Graham, enlist in the Corps. In 1952, Second Lieutenant Frank E. Petersen, Jr. (later Lieutenant General) became the first black aviator in the Marine Corps, who then went on to become the first black Marine general in 1979. In 2012, the Montford Point Marines were awarded the Congressional Gold Medal. Montford Point is now known as Camp Gilbert H. Johnson, after "Hashmark" Johnson.

For over a year, Walter's life was spent at sea in the South Pacific where one day was the same as the next; Monday was no different from Saturday. The sun's heat glistening off the water was hot. An occasional rain was a welcome relief, but the balmy breezes didn't blow often enough. On occasion, Walter must have thought about what it was like back in Miami. Though Miami's weather was likewise always hot and humid, the temperature did cool some during the winter months. The rainy season filled Lake Okeechobee and allowed all the vegetation to flourish. Would he live to see it again? He was no different from the rest of his shipmates. They wanted revenge for Pearl Harbor by giving the Japanese a shellacking they'd never forget; one that would cause them to surrender so "we could all go home." They prayed they would live through the war, and one day go home to resume their lives with family and friends. They had answered the call and anxiously anticipated the next chapter of their lives. Lest we forget, our nation can never thank these brave men and women enough for their exceptional bravery and sacrifices.

Once the *Portland* was repaired at Mare Island, she participated in an operational training exercise (often referred to as a shakedown cruise after significant repairs had been accomplished to ensure the ship was battle ready) off the coast of Southern California. From there she sailed for the Aleutian Islands, where she bombarded Kiska Island, and then covered a reconnaissance landing on Little Kiska Island. Leaving those fog-bound waters, she went to Pearl Harbor, then back to San Francisco in early October, returning again to Pearl in mid-October. November saw her returning to the fight in the South Pacific, receiving a "well done" in the Gilbert and Marshall Island campaigns, where she suffered but one loss. One of her scout planes failed to return from an anti-submarine patrol.

Next, her mission was again screening carriers engaged in battles on Palau, Yap, Ulithi and Woleai. Four of her men were wounded by Japanese attack planes, but she suffered no fatalities. From there she sailed with another carrier force covering the landing on New Guinea and air strikes on Truk before accompanying five other cruisers and destroyers to bombard Satawan. After this series of island operations, the *Portland* sailed for Mare Island where she received a complete overhaul before returning to the Western Pacific.

The long months of constant combat, day after day and night after night of attacking or being attacked, and fearing he could be killed at any moment, had taken not only a physical, but more damaging, a mental toll on Walter as battle fatigue enveloped his mind and body. R&R in Australia had helped, but treatment of a different kind seemed warranted. His commander, in concert with the ship's doctor, determined Walter was temporarily unfit for duty. He suffered from what the doctor described as 60 percent disabling battle fatigue, today known as post traumatic stress disorder, or PTSD. Treatment required relief from the combat environment; Walter was given a fourteen-day leave. *Just what the doctor ordered,* thought Walter. He headed straight to Miami. He and Ethel, who hadn't seen each other since Walter shipped out more than a year earlier, were married March 13, 1943. After his leave was up, he brought Ethel with him to the West Coast where he found a

Walter and Ethel cutting wedding cake, March 13, 1943

cottage for her in Vallejo, California, before returning to the *Portland*. Permanent changes of station (PCS) orders were in the works seeking a duty assignment for him out of the combat arena. On May 19, 1943, Walter received orders leaving his beloved "Sweet Pea," directing him to report for duty as an instructor at the Navy Supply Corps School, Harvard Graduate School of Business Administration in Boston. His personnel file indicates that on May 14, he received dependent transportation for Ethel in the form of a lower berth train ticket from 124 Olympic Street, Chabot Terrace, Vallejo, California to 15 Linnean Street, Cambridge, Massachusetts. Apparently Walter had gone ahead to Boston and obtained lodging for Ethel, as she was not prone to going anywhere until she knew her exact destination.

Newlyweds leaving for California, March 17, 1948

While at the Supply School, Walter's PTSD worsened, and his commanding officer encouraged him to seek treatment. Many military personnel suffering from this ailment refuse treatment, viewing it as a sign of weakness. Whether that was Walter's thinking at the time we do not know, but he did not seek professional help. Possibly he decided to deal with it himself as he typically handled any difficulty in life that came his way. As the years passed, he was in no way visibly disabled, but the war had changed Walter. Just serving in the military changes one, and serving in combat is equally recognized. In 1954, during a routine physical, the Navy doctor noted "psyche disturbance of nervousness and sequelae," or aftereffect of an illness or injury, for which he was granted a waiver if he was later ordered back on active duty. Walter had an incurable ailment, one that could only be treated, not necessarily cured. He dealt with it in his own way for the rest of his life.

Ethel, circa 1945

Feeling a need to find something for Ethel to occupy her time while he was at work, Walter found her a receptionist/administrative job in the Psychology Department at Harvard. Within months Ethel became pregnant, requiring her to quit her job because she was at high risk. On July 4, 1938, she had received substantial injuries in a very serious car accident, and was told she may never be able to bear children. Fortunately, Walter could be with her during this time. He would remain at the Supply Corps School until April 29, 1945. But while Walter and Ethel were enjoying their time together, the war went on, and would produce many other heroes.

In the spring of 1944, a very young naval aviator was about to engage the Japanese in the skies over the Pacific. As soon as George H. W. Bush graduated from the Phillips Academy in Massachusetts at age eighteen, he delayed going to college, enlisted in the Navy, and was accepted in flight school. Ten months later he was commissioned an ensign as the youngest pilot in the Navy. Within months, he was assigned to Torpedo Squadron VT-51 aboard the aircraft carrier USS *San Jacinto*, piloting a Gruman TBM Avenger. The Avenger was the heaviest single engine bomber in the war, with a crew of three—pilot, radio/bombardier, and turret gunner. Shortly thereafter, his Air Group 51 was fighting in the Battle for the Philippines, second in magnitude only to the Battle of Midway.

During an early operation, then Lieutenant Junior Grade Bush was credited with sinking a small Japanese cargo ship before making a forced water landing. On September 2, Bush and three other planes attacked Japanese shore installations on the island of Chi Chi Jima. Encountering heavy anti-aircraft fire during their attack, Bush was able to release all four of his bombs on target, but he was hit. His engine was on fire, spouting flames, and smoke obscuring his vision. Still, he flew several miles away from the island before he and one of his crew bailed out. Both his crew were ultimately determined to have been killed in action, the second crew member presumed to have died in the plane from enemy gun fire. Four hours later, Bush was rescued by a submarine, the USS *Finback*. For his actions, Bush received the Distinguished Flying Cross, and, of course, went on to become the 41st president of the United States. He joined the ranks as yet another American war hero of the Greatest Generation.

Bombing Japan

It was during this time in April 1944, that General "Hap" Arnold, commanding general of the Army Air Corps, sent his first B-29 Superfortress long-range bombers to bomb Japan and Japanese facilities elsewhere in Southeast Asia. Initially his bombers, and their P-51 Mustang escort fighters, flew out of bases in India, but the distance was prohibitive. Within a month they were flying out of Saipan, Guam, and Tinian, which were only 1,500 miles from mainland Japan.

On one of the B-29s named "Jack's Hack," flight engineer Technical Sergeant Henry Chodacki recalls sitting in his seat behind the copilot, facing the tail, for the normal fifteen-hour mission. The mission involved flying from Tinian to Japan via Iwo Jima, while the bombardier/nose gunner, positioned below and in front of the pilot and copilot, dropped their incendiary bombs on industrial and military targets, including communication, manufacturing, and transportation sites in Tokyo and Yokohoma. They would then return to Tinian to do it all over again a day or two later. Henry told this author the to and from flights were boring, which gave him more time to ponder why his seat had to face the tail, and the rest of the crew faced forward, except for the tail gunner, who also faced the tail. The flights were always in danger of being shot at by Japanese Zeroes and other fighters, so they often flew above 30,000 feet and at speeds of up to 350 mph, both of which exceeded the capabilities of the Zeroes. Flying at such heights required all crew members to wear leather shearling-lined helmets, jackets, pants, gloves, and calf-high boots to keep warm. The real danger came when they dropped down low to 7,000-8,000 feet on their bombing runs. That's where they were most vulnerable. The bombings became known as fire raids, as each bomber dropped 20,000 pounds of incendiary bombs, designed to blow up on impact and start fires. This was when the P-51s and Japanese fighters engaged in dogfights all around and above the bombers. Anti-aircraft guns were blazing and their flak bursts were scary because one couldn't see them coming through the ack-ack bursts and smoke. Of the 3,970 B-29 bombers built between 1943 and 1945, almost all saw action bombing Japan. Every crewman just did his job and counted the successful flights, praying to reach the magic twenty-five flights, which gave him his ticket out of combat or maybe even home. The odds, however, were not good. It was not unusual for flights of several hundred planes to leave Saipan and Tinian every day. With that many planes in the air it is no surprise that 450 were shot down, carrying 568 crew members. If they were going down it was best to ditch in the water and hope to be picked up, rather than crash on land, as the Japanese were sure to capture you. Of those who did go down, most plane crew captives were sent to the Ofuna POW Camp near Yokohoma. The Ofuna Camp was where high-value enlisted and officers, particularly pilots and submariners, were held to be tortured and interrogated. Such prisoners were thought to have more information about Allied operations than a foot soldier or sailor deckhand. Many prisoners died from the beatings and torture, as well as being unable to survive on 500 calories of food per day. Malnutrition caused other ailments to set in. Failure of body organs, teeth, and hair falling out were not uncommon. Most unfortunately, nearly half of them never survived the POW camp. Japan was not a signatory on the 1929 Geneva Convention for POWs. Some were beheaded, beaten, used for bayonet practice, or otherwise physically abused for the sheer enjoyment of the Japanese guards. At best, they were used as slave laborers. Two of the most famous prisoners, both of whom did survive, were Louis Zamperini (1936 Olympic distance runner) of the book, *Unbroken,* fame, and Marine pilot Major "Pappy" Boyington. Boyington was a Medal of Honor recipient, commander of the Black Sheep Squadron, and fighter Ace. Before being shot down and captured, he shot down twenty-six Japanese planes. The Japanese government has never apologized for the abuses inflicted on the American POWS, only acknowledging it happened.

Another Marine who served with the 1st Marine Division during the Battles of Peliliu and Okinawa was a Quaker, Paul Douglas. He joined the Marine Corps in 1942, becoming the oldest man to ever go through Marine boot camp at the age of fifty. During combat, because of his religious beliefs, Douglas was assigned to carry ammunition to the front lines, which earned him two purple hearts and a bronze star, for killing one Japanese soldier. He was discharged a lieutenant colonel with full disability as a result of a burst of Japanese machine gun fire that left his left arm hang limply for the rest of his life. Douglas later became a U.S. senator from Illinois. While serving three terms in the Senate, he was a staunch advocate for equal rights, and just as strong an opponent of pork barrel. It is amazing how members of Congress still love their pork barrel.

Sen. Paul Douglas and author, Toys for Tots campaign
1957, Rockford, Illinois

During WWII, the English-born American comedian, Bob Hope, felt duty bound to do his part in support of the American fighting forces. Working with the United Service Organizations (USO), he performed his first USO show for our troops at March Field (later renamed March Air Force Base) in California on May 6, 1941. It was a big hit and he told the USO he wanted to do shows where the troops were fighting. There were serious security problems to surmount, but Hope was determined to go where the troops were. He wanted to give them some comic relief to lift their spirits and make them smile and laugh. Oftentimes he was performing so close to the front lines that the sounds of guns and rockets firing could be heard on the stage. He sure boosted troop morale for decades to come though, spending almost thirty of those years overseas with the troops during the Christmas holidays. His 57th and last USO tour was in 1988. Always accompanying him on all his tours was his beloved wife, Dolores, and a group of famous entertainers, including musicians, movie stars, singers, and athletes.

One such tour in the South Pacific was on the islands of Banika and Pavuvu in the Solomon Islands. While appearing on Banika, a Special Services Marine officer told Hope the 1st Marine Division was training on the secret island Pavuvu, some seven miles distant, in preparation for invading Peliliu. All Hope said was, "How do we get there?" He was told there was no runway on the island and the only way was to fly in by Piper Cub and land on a dirt road. Hope said, "We'll be ready tomorrow." The following day actress Frances Langford, dancer Patty Thomas, gag-writer Barney Dean, comedian Jerry Colonna, singer Tony Romano, and Bob (carrying his ever-present golf club in his hand) were loaded one person per plane and pilot, arriving on Pavuvu in a matter of minutes. They gave the Marines one helluva surprise show. As was always the case, wounded were in the front row. Stopping to speak with one of the Marines who had stuck out his hand, Hope, seeing the transfusion in the kid's arm quipped, "I see they're giving you a little pick-me-up." The Marine smiled and said, "It was only raspberry soda, but it feels pretty good." Two hours later a doctor informed Hope the Marine had died. During the fierce battle on

Peliliu, 1,800 of the Marines Hope entertained on Pavuvu died. During his time in the Pacific, Hope traveled more than 30,000 miles giving over 150 performances for those who were fighting to keep Japan from reaching U.S. soil. Among his many awards and recognitions, Bob Hope received the Congressional Gold Medal from President John F. Kennedy, and the Presidential Medal of Freedom from President Lyndon B. Johnson. The English comedian was a great American.

BOMBING BERLIN

In 1944, three years after the war in the Pacific had begun, and a year before Walter left the Navy Supply School at Harvard returning to the Pacific, the U.S. involvement in the war in Europe had just begun. The United States was bombing targets in Europe, including Germany. One such group of airmen was Crew 9, 752nd Squadron, 458th Bombardment Group (H), led by pilot and this author's cousin, then-First Lieutenant Joseph "Joe" Roubal.

Pilot 2nd Lt Joseph W. Roubal
(second from left, top row)
with his #9 crew

Joseph William Roubal was born in 1915 in the coal mining town of White City, Illinois, the only son of Mary and William Roubal. Mary Hrebik Roubal, my aunt, was born in Bohemia, Austro-Hungarian Empire (now the Czech Republic), arriving in America in 1903 with my grandparents. When Joe left Mount Olive High School after only three years in 1927, he started working in the #15 Consolidated Coal Company mine with his father and uncles. But digging below the earth's surface was not what Mary wanted for Joe, and everyday life was even worse during the ten years of the Great Depression. It is not known when Joe left White City, but he soon found his way to the southwest, working in New Mexico and Nevada. As the war in the Pacific raged on, Joe saw an opportunity to better himself and serve his country, which he loved with a passion; a country he was fully prepared to fight and die for, if necessary.

458th Bomber Group over Germany, 1944

Shortly after completing Army Air Corps flight school, Joe and his crew joined the 458th Bombardment Group on October 20, 1943, in Tonopah, Nevada. Tonopah, which lies in the middle of the desert midway between Las Vegas and Reno, was an old rundown gold and silver mining town at the time. It saw a resurgence in 1979, and gold is again actively mined there today.

Joe and his crew immediately received advanced bomber combat crew training, which was just what they were hoping for. They were going to go bomb either the Japs or the Germans. They didn't care which; they just wanted to get into the war before it was over. Two months later the tall lanky pilot, then-Second Lieutenant Joe Roubal, and his crew were ordered to fly the southern route to the Royal Air Force Base, Horsham St Faith in England, via Hamilton Field, California, and a yet-to-be-identified airfield in Florida. They were flying the brand new B-24H Liberators, the heaviest lift bomber designed to date for the war in Europe. Known as "flying boxcars' because of their shape and the massive amount of bombs they carried, they were also disparagingly referred to as "flying coffins."The reason for the deadly moniker was because the only way in and out of the aircraft was in the rear. Should a plane be shot down it was highly unlikely the pilot, co-pilot, and nose gunner would have time to maneuver through the small tunnel to the rear of the aircraft—with parachutes strapped to their backs—and jump, before hitting the ground. Joe's plane proudly displayed an image of the Statue of Liberty and was aptly named "Liberty Lib" on the side of her fuselage.

Arriving at RAF Horsham in late January 1944, five months before D-Day on Normandy, they flew orientation flights learning the topography of the land, locations of Allied and German forces, and potential targets. On their first combat mission over Germany on March 3, Liberty Lib dropped fifty-two M47 incendiary bombs on target. During the attack, Joe observed several other bombers being shot down, including that of a friend, Second Lieutenant (2dLt) Guy Rogers. Joe's emotional report reads: "B-24 with K on it first seen about 18,000, circled down with #2 engine smoking, five parachutes opened and plane crashed just over lake SW of Berlin at 1344 hours." In addition to their personal names and decorations, the planes had very large letters and/or numbers on their fuselage for distant identification. The "K" Joe saw identified the plane as 2dLt Rogers'. With a crew of ten, it meant five went down with the plane. Liberty Lib was identified as 7V. On March 6, 1944, taking on his third combat mission over German forces in Europe, he was about to initiate the first successful American bombing raid on the city of Berlin. Flying to the left of group leader Colonel Isbell, Joe and his crew witnessed several other aircraft being shot down around them by German anti-aircraft batteries. While his gunners were kept busy shooting at the German fighters attacking them, Liberty Lib succeeded in dropping all fifty-two of her incendiary bombs on target that day, returning to base with just a reasonable number of bullet holes. In addition to all bombs landing on Berlin, Liberty Lib was credited with shooting down one German fighter. All members of the crew, except Technical Sergeant (TSgt) Dailey, were awarded the Distinguished Flying Cross, and recognized as follows:

Captain Joseph Roubal...pilot
First Lieutenant Arnold LeHardy ....co-pilot
First Lieutenant John Ekberg .... navigator
First Lieutenant James Trent ....bombardier
Technical Sergeant William Dailey ....radio operator
Staff Sergeant Edward Fitzgerald .... flight engineer

Technical Sergeant Norman Holm ....waist gunner
Staff Sergeant Gordon Carlson......................................waist gunner
Staff Sergeant James McKanna.................... ball turret (belly) gunner
Staff Sergeant Donald Henry ....tail gunner

Joe and all his number 9 crew flew Liberty Lib on twelve more combat missions before being assigned to several other Liberators. By August 4, Roubal had completed thirty-two missions (seven more than the required twenty-five combat missions), and was assigned ground duties as the Squadron's operations officer. Joe had obviously volunteered for more combat duty than was required of him. By the end of operations over Germany, the approximate 200 planes and 2,000 crew of the 458th Bombardment Group suffered the following loses:

- 47 aircraft lost
- 179 personnel KIA
- 125 personnel died in accidents
- 193 became POWs
- 33 evaded capture
- 60 were sheltered and hidden by neutral countries

Two that were captured were murdered by German police, and their murderers were brought to justice after the war. The murderers of Sergeant James Murray, crew member of "Top of the Mark" were never caught.

But Joe wasn't done yet. He stayed on in Germany after the war, brought his wife, Jean, over from the States, and flew in the Berlin Airlift. He described his emotions to me as very mixed when bringing food and supplies to people he had bombed just months earlier. Such are the vagaries of war.

Returning to the States, Joe was assigned to the Los Alamos National Laboratory in New Mexico, a region of the country with which he was most familiar. Joe never spoke about what work he was doing at Los Alamos, nor about Area 51 in Nevada. He just said it was all TOP SECRET stuff. When asked about UFOs and aliens, he just said "I can't talk about that stuff either."

Whether the memories of Germany or his work at Los Alamos caused the alcohol demons to invade his body, we don't know. The last time I saw Joe was at my mother's funeral in 1949. Two years later he sent me my first tuxedo shirt for my sixteenth birthday. Within a few years, Joe retired from the U.S. Air Force (formerly Army Air Corps), and moved his wife and daughter, Sharon, to Oklahoma. Soon after, Joe went back to the desert to deal with his demons, somewhat as Pima Indian Marine Corporal Ira Hayes (one of the flag raisers on Iwo Jima) did. When the deserts of our southwest didn't help, Joe went to Mexico and worked on a road gang, believing the manual labor under a blistering sun would cure him. In 1958, he died in a Tucson hospital from cirrhosis of the liver. Joe, another true war hero of the Greatest Generation is buried in the Fort Rosecrans National Cemetery in San Diego.

The least heralded branch of the military services in WWII was the Women's Airforce Service Pilots (WASP). Talk about freeing a man to fight, these women were on the top of the list, even above Rosie the Riveter. With all the male pilots committed to combat roles, there was a dire need for trained and licensed pilots to test some of the new planes coming out of the manufacturing plants, and to ferry them to various airbases around the country. Jacqueline (Jackie) Cochran, the best female pilot in America at the time, and friend Amelia Earhart, contacted Eleanor Roosevelt, wife of President Franklin Delano Roosevelt, proposing the formation of a women's flying service to help during WWII. Jackie certainly had all the qualifications to start and lead such a unit; she was a top racing pilot during the 1930s who had already volunteered for, and flown with, the British Royal Air Force in Europe. Authorized on July 1, 1943, the organization was initially titled Women's Army Corps (WAC). As director of the new service, Jackie went around the country quickly enlisting 25,000 women. Of the 25,000, only 1,074 made it through physical examinations and flight training. Their pilot training in Houston and Sweetwater, Texas, was the same as that of male pilots. Soon after graduating and receiving their wings, the new WASPs were in the skies over America, much to the regret and disdain of many men.

One of those first pilots was Lorraine Rogers. Lorraine learned to fly at Orchard Field, a small grass runway airstrip outside Chicago now known as O'Hare International Airport. (O'Hare Airport is named after yet another naval aviator, Lieutenant Commander Edward "Butch" O'Hare. O'Hare was the Navy's first WWII flying ace who further distinguished himself in battle by receiving the Medal of Honor. On November 26, 1943, while flying an F-6F Hellcat night dive-bombing mission off the USS *Enterprise,* he was shot down in a dog fight with Japanese fighter/bombers. Neither he nor his plane was ever found.)

One day during Lorraine's flight training, her instructor told her to take a solo practice run. Shortly after takeoff her plane flipped over; all of her learned skills to bring it out of a flat spin failed. She parachuted out, again following all the instructions to the letter, including "count to ten before pulling the ripcord." She did not have much altitude, so she took the instructions literally, cleverly said "one to ten" and pulled. She had some cuts and bruises and thought the board of inquiry would wash her out, but it didn't. After the inquiry, her instructor told her "Your rudder cables had been cut," but they never told her who did it. She was soon flying seven days a week. The typical day would be to pick up a new plane just off the assembly line in Kansas City, take it up, test it, and accept it for the Army Air Corps. Then she would chart her course for delivery, say to California, take off and be on her own, landing and refueling wherever she chose along the way until she reached her delivery field. (It is possible, but never verified, Lorraine may have ferried the Liberty Lib to Hamilton Field, where Joe Roubal picked it up.) There were incidents of not being recognized by the tower when seeking landing instructions, and having refueling crews walk away when she took off her helmet revealing her long wavy hair. Each of these incidents required her to complain to the base commander, showing her orders and ID in order to get her plane serviced. Like all the other WASPs, she persevered and just did her job.

By war's end, the original 1,074 WASPs flew over 60,000 hours in fighters and bombers; thirty-eight of them died in service. On December 20, 1944, they were disbanded by an unappreciative U.S. Congress and forgotten. Their records were classified and sealed for thirty-five years before finally being recognized by Congress as military veterans and awarded their service medals.

The strongest lobbying efforts were provided by another former ferry pilot, Senator Barry Goldwater. Lorraine Rogers was there at the hearing and observed one senator hit his desk with his fist saying, "Over my dead body will those prima donnas get veterans status" and stormed out. In 2010, President Barack Obama and Congress awarded the WASP the Congressional Gold Medal.

As one who may well have watched Joe Roubal fly overhead later in the war, then six-year-old Mike Trubuil remembers well June 30, 1940, the day the German Army invaded the Channel Islands in the English Channel between England and France. The islands were the only part of the United Kingdom ever occupied by the Nazi forces in WWII. Mike and his family had always lived on Guernsey, the second largest island in the chain. It is only twenty-three miles from the French coast, yet seventy-three miles from its homeland.

Mike's father told the family that trucks had been sent to transport all school-age children, and any adults who chose to evacuate to St. Peter Port Harbor. From there they would board ships loaded with tomatoes bound for England, *but you have to move quickly, no time to pack,* his father said. Young Mike heard the German Dornier Do 17 bombers bombing the first trucks, killing forty-four islanders, and wondered what would happen next. (The Dornier Do was better known as the "flying pencils" because the fuselage behind the cockpit was pencil thin, which created a very small target for the English anti-aircraft guns to hit.) The unknown was scary; even more so for a young boy. Unfortunately, Mike was not among the 17,000 islanders who managed to evacuate, as he had missed the last boat. School was suspended, as all the nuns had evacuated. Mike's life changed dramatically in less than one hour's time. Only 21,000 islanders remained on Guernsey, and there were no English soldiers to defend the island. Several days later, many German Junker Transport planes landed on the island airport disgorging roughly 17,000 German troops to occupy the island.

Being a cobbler, Mr. Trubuil was allowed to continue his trade instead of being assigned to build bunkers for the German defense lines. Many soldiers came daily to have their boots repaired. In time, Mike's father had so much business two Algerian POWs were assigned to help him keep up with the demand. As the kids in town grew used to the German soldiers, who often joked and played around with them, the kids stopped being so afraid. Almost daily, as the soldiers marched into or out of town, the kids surrounded them clapping and cheering. Or, if they felt mischievous, they'd fall in line behind the soldiers and mimic their marching. Such playing was somewhat annoying to the soldiers, but they never did anything more than to shoo the kids out of their way. A year later school resumed in churches, as the German soldiers occupied the school buildings. Many islanders soon learned how to assemble crystal radio sets in order to hear the latest news of the war from London. Ingenuity turned lead from pencils, fine wire, a nail, table lamp cord, and a small headset into a simple, but effective radio—which was hidden during the day, and brought out secretly at night when the soldiers weren't nearby. Food was increasingly in short supply for both the islanders and the soldiers, so various forms of rationing were applied to help avoid malnutrition or other ailments related to the lack of sufficient food.

Four years after the Germans had first arrived on Guernsey, in March 1944, Mike first heard and saw American bombers flying west over Guernsey, taking a southerly route over France north to Germany. The bombers only flew at night, attempting to reduce their visual vulnerability. But the Germans had huge searchlights in the harbor shining up into the sky, affording the anti-aircraft batteries opportunities to shoot down the bombers. The noise of the shells flying overhead scared Mike and the other islanders, and they sometimes even felt pieces of shrapnel fall from the sky when a plane had been hit.

Finally, mid-morning on May 9, 1945, then nine-year-old Mike and the rest of the students watched a school teacher enter the classroom saying, "You can all go home—the war's over." In the days that followed, the German soldiers were made to dig up all the land mines they had placed on the beaches before they were shipped off the island for processing as POWs. Young Mike's war was finally over. Today, Mike and his beautiful wife, Joan, are retired from a very successful landscaping business, and still live happily on Guernsey when they're not cruising and traveling around the world.

WALTER RETURNS TO THE PACIFIC

When Lieutenant Beckham was ordered to report to the submarine tender USS *Sperry* (AS-12) on May 19, 1945, the war in Europe had just ended eleven days earlier on May 8. The war in the Pacific, however, still raged on, and Walter was back in it. Ethel and their first child, Barbara, born in Boston, went to split

Walter, Ethel, and baby Barbara

their time living with each of their parents. It is noted Walter and Ethel were miraculously blessed with Barbara's birth, because Ethel was thought to be unable to bear children as a result of a serious automobile accident years earlier. Walter sent a message to his "little girl," Barbara, every night. As the years past, Barbara grew to become the apple of his eye, often to the chagrin of her younger brothers,

who seemed to always come in second and third to their big sister in affection from dad. The feelings were true, as Walter treated girls different than boys.

The *Sperry* was refitting and repairing submarines at Majuro Atoll in the Marshall Islands, while the Navy and Marines were fighting the Battle of Okinawa, the largest amphibious assault of the war in the Pacific. On June 30, the *Sperry* sailed west and slightly north toward Japan, stopping at Guam in the Marianas. While on Guam, Walter was placed in charge of a group of three officers who were given a very detailed one-day pass by the island provost marshal, Marine Colonel Victor A. Barraco. Their pass was to go sight-seeing (not liberty) through the native community, provided they check in and out with each community chief patrolman. It also admonished them to "forbid trading or bartering with natives, consumption, sale, or purchase of alcoholic beverages and beer, and observe all other regulations in effect regarding the conduct of military personnel."

In October, the Bureau of Naval Personnel (BuPers) determined Walter was eligible for release from active duty effective September 13, 1945. Walter was still looking for his ticket to go home. On October 3, he was promoted to the rank of lieutenant commander, receiving a $100 uniform gratuity to add the proper rank insignias on his sleeves and epaulets. Though appreciative of the promotion, Walter was more interested in being released from active duty as the Navy indicated was to have happened the previous month. To his dismay, his commanding officer saw fit to dispute the orders from BuPers. Instead, his commanding officer wrote to BuPers stating Walter could not be released from active duty until a suitable replacement was provided meeting a long list of qualifications including "Duties of a supply officer on a large submarine tender at an advanced base…and additional duties requiring supervision of supply functions and disbursing duties for all submarine activities in this advanced area…were extremely important to the operation of a large submarine tender, requiring the talents of an experienced Supply/Disbursing Officer." Initially, Walter was to be retained on active duty more than ninety days awaiting a suitable replacement. Walter signed a statement that was sent to the chief of naval personnel requesting "I be relieved as soon as practicable in order that I may continue my professional education, which was interrupted when I was called to active duty." Walter was busy trying to coordinate his plan to return to civilian life and school. An interesting aside to his journey appears in his personnel file, which I obtained through a Freedom of Information request from the National Personnel Records Center in St. Louis. For reasons known only to him, on November 27, Walter requested and was given permission to visit the Republic of Cuba, staying in the Nacional Hotel Havana, during the period January 22-31, 1946, provided he wore mufti (civilian clothes). It is unclear whether or not Walter ever went to Cuba. What's most intriguing is he planned to complete the travel to Cuba after he was detached from the *Sperry* on December 22, 1945. Though V-J Day was August 14, Walter's war did not end until December 22. Nine years later Walter requested permission to take a similar trip to eleven European countries. His request contained a very detailed day-by-day itinerary including air, sea, rail, and hotel reservations. Though initially approved by the commandant of the Sixth Naval District, his trip was later canceled by the same commandant without explanation. The purposes for the trips to Cuba and Europe are known only to Walter. His final journey home was about to begin. First he reported to the Naval Staging Center on Guam, on December 22, for transportation back to the States. Arriving January 9, 1946 at the Personnel Intake Station established at Camp Elliott, San Diego, Walter received orders on January 17 to further report to the Personnel Separation Center, Naval Air Station in Jacksonville, Florida on January 18. He was granted a 105-day leave, marched out the door, and returned on May 3. Finally, he would be officially released from active duty later that day. He had served four years, ten months and ten days, but his service to his country was not over. Though he declined a letter from the Navy Department of Supplies and Accounts to return to active duty and make the Navy a career, he remained active in the Naval Reserve, earning all credits required annually by attending drills, completing extension educational courses, and summer periods of active duty, sometimes aboard ship, until on April 18, 1980, Captain Walter H. Beckham Jr. officially retired from the Navy. His awards received are:

- Navy Unit Commendation
- Combat Action Ribbon
- American Defense Medal
- American Theatre Campaign Medal
- Asiatic-Pacific Campaign Medal w/6 stars
- World War II Victory Medal
- Armed Forces Reserve Medal

On September 2, 1945, Walter's former ship, the USS *Portland*, was designated the flagship for Vice Admiral George Murray, who represented Admiral Nimitz at the ceremony in which Japanese Navy Vice Admiral Chuichi Hara, Commander, 4th Fleet, signed the documents surrendering the Japanese base on Truk Island in the Caroline Islands. Walter would have been proud to witness the event, but he was then serving aboard the USS *Sperry*. Soon after, "Sweet Pea" participated in Operation Magic Carpet, bringing 600 troops home to the West Coast. From there, she sailed through the Panama Canal and twice brought troops home from Europe. In July 1946, the *Portland* was "mothballed" as part of the Reserve Fleet at the Philadelphia Navy Yard. On March 1, 1959, the magnificent lady was stricken from the Navy Registry, and on October 6, she was sold for scrap to the Union Mineral and Alloys Corporation of New York, New York.

In 1945, the United States and the Soviet Union military forces decided the future of Korea. In an emergency meeting, then Army Colonel Dean Rusk drew a line on the map along the 38th parallel. American forces occupied the southern part of the peninsula, and Soviet troops occupied the northern part. Less than five years later a dispute over the line caused North and South Korea to go to war, which pulled in troops from the United Nations, including the United States, Russia, and China. Border lines between nations will forever be disputed.

AZORIAN/GLOMAR PROJECT

Some twenty years after the end of WWII, the island of Midway would again be a focal point in the Cold War. During the summer of 1974, at an estimated cost of $800 million, the Azorian/Glomar Project (recently declassified) involved using the specially reconfigured *Hughes Glomar Explorer* ship to raise the Soviet Submarine K-129, which sank near Midway Island in 1968. Soon after the K-129 sank, the USS *Halibut,* a guided missile submarine, located the K-129 on the ocean floor and photographed it. The K-129 was believed to be carrying three R-21 nuclear missiles and numerous highly classified cryptological documents and equipment. If the sub was raised, all the nuclear material had to be stored in special bunkers designed for such storage. Midway was to be the "storage" site. First, quite a bit of work went into preparing the facility to house the HOT (radioactive) material. The channel had to be dredged leading to the fuel pier, and the bunkers rehabbed. The island, in fact, was already being used to store U.S. nuclear warheads from American nuclear submarines when they were not on routine patrol duties in Soviet waters. Fortunately, Midway was never used for the project as only a portion of the Soviet submarine was recovered; it broke apart during the raising efforts. All that was recovered were two nuclear torpedoes and six crewmen, who received proper military burial at sea in metal caskets, due to radioactive material exposure.

CHAPTER 7

PROFESSOR AND LAWYER

The year 1945 was a seminal year in Walter's life. After almost five years active duty in the Navy, he could finally begin the next phase of his life, that being a legal career. His plan included remaining active in the Navy Reserves, eventually receiving a modicum of retirement income for him and Ethel, to supplement what income he anticipated receiving as a highly successful lawyer. In a qualifications questionnaire he completed some years later, he stated his first real civilian job was that of a real estate salesman for three months in 1946. Grants in profession often started on the lowest rung of the ladder.

While attending Harvard Law School, Walter received a James A. Rumrill Scholarship, which helped defray his college expenses. While there, he stood above others receiving the honorary distinctions of being editor, *Harvard Law Review*, being a member of the Board of Student Advisors, the Harvard Legal Aid Bureau, and the Scott Law Club.

Professor Walter H. Beckham Jr.

Walter H. Beckham III, their second child, was born in 1948, the year Walter graduated with an LLB law degree *cum laude*. Needing full-time employment to provide for a growing family, he returned to Miami in an old car he hand-painted himself and $50 in his pocket. He became an associate professor of law at the University of Miami (UM) Law School until 1951, where he also served as a faculty advisor for the UM *Law Quarterly* from 1948-1949. He received an annual salary of somewhere between $3,500 and $5,000. From then on his curriculum vitae reads like an extremely busy and successful lawyer, which he was—maybe even a Don Quixote—while still managing to help Ethel raise their three children. With all the time required in carrying out his enormous workload, Walter still managed to take his children to school every day on his way to work, and he somehow managed to be home for dinner between 6:00 or 6:15 every weekday evening. All family members were expected to be seated by 6:30. Discussions, typically led by Walter, were about the activities of each person that day, be it good or bad, including the occasional argument between the parents. Ethel "ran" the house, but Walter "ruled" the house. Children, as was the common practice in those days, sat at the table until they finished everything on their plate, period. Only homework might allow someone to escape with food still on his or her plate. There was no watching television on weeknights, and telephone calls were frowned on. Bedtime was 9:00 until the eighth grade. From then on the reins were slightly loosened, dependent particularly on grades. No one had better ever bring home anything less than As or Bs on their report cards. By high school, Pop beat everyone to bed, falling fast asleep by 9:30 or 10 o'clock.

With Walter busy growing his law career, Ethel was busy in her own right, giving of herself to help others in any way she could. When Walter was asked to join the school board he declined; Ethel immediately said she would, and did. She was very active in civic affairs and passionate about educating the young, evidenced by having the Ethel Koger Beckham Elementary School in Miami named after her. For the rest of her life she cared dearly for her students, visiting the school frequently to ensure they were receiving the very best education possible.

Walter III tells the story of one of those nights. "It was a wonderful spring evening so I had my door and windows open to enjoy the fresh air, and I was smoking a cigar, which I had been doing since fourth or fifth grade. I heard mom unlocking and opening the door at the top of the back stairway which led down to my room. She said, 'Your father smells smoke—are you smoking a cigar?' to which I replied, 'Yes ma'am.'

"After a long pause she said, 'Well please don't burn the house down.'

'Yes ma'am.'

"The door was closed and relocked. Both my parents generally showed good judgment as to which fights to pick and which ones were better left alone."

On another occasion when young Walter had snuck out at night, all three of his re-entry plans were blocked, but brother Jimmy came through and helped him get back in. The next morning, being a Saturday, Walter always made breakfast for the family. When young Walter came down and entered the kitchen, Walter inquired, "Good morning, how did you sleep?"

"Great, thanks," replied young Walter. He knew his father knew about the night before and there was nothing to be gained by scolding him. It was just another example of the extraordinary wisdom displayed by Walter Beckham.

DEMONSTRATIVE EVIDENCE

The following year Walter joined the law firm of Dixon, DeJarnette, and Bradford while continuing to teach nights at UM. 1950 saw him join another firm, Nichols, Gaither & Green, which later became Nichols, Gaither, Beckham, Colson, Spence & Hicks when Walter was made partner in 1952, and where he would remain until the firm dissolved in 1967. The Nichols Gaither firm occupied its own million dollar circular law office building at 1111 Brickell Avenue in Miami.

Perry Nichols' law firm round office building, Miami, Florida

By now the firm had four offices in four cities, employing over 100 people. The firm employed a team of investigators to assist the lawyers in preparing their cases. Unique still today, Nichols had a doctor and nurse on staff to care for his lawyers and staff, in addition to conducting medical-related research and appearing as expert witnesses at trials. There was a gas pump in the parking lot for lawyers and staff to fill up their cars, and runners to handle personal needs of the staff such as dropping off or picking up cleaning, or delivering documents, etc., to the courthouse or other law offices. All this was designed to keep the staff at work behind their desks as much of the time as possible, day and night, seven days a week, if necessary.

This was when and where the use of demonstrative evidence tactics in a trial were invented by Walter and the firm's founder, Perry Nichols. Their offices housed an extensive medical library, photographer and a darkroom, visual aids, and movies related to cases. Courtrooms were soon filled with charts, diagrams, pictures, graphs, blueprints, surveys, and actual objects relating to cases—something never before seen by judges or jurors. Perry was a former insurance company adjustor who decided he could make more money going up against the insurance companies on behalf of individual plaintiffs seeking damages from various injuries or death sustained in myriad accidents. And he was right. He knew how the enemy operated, which enabled him to defeat them frequently. Perry and Walter literally changed the normally accepted practices applied in the courtroom. Engaging primarily in personal injury cases, demonstrative evidence clearly, and often graphically, displayed the gravity and extent of injuries to the defendant insurance companies. Of course, the initial challenges were to obtain acceptance of this practice by the courts. Walter explained it this way, "Plaintiffs deserved greater compensation for pain and suffering than was customarily offered by the insurance companies. And as the world was becoming more technically complex, judges and juries needed to be educated on the difference between verbally saying a leg had been severed in a train accident, and showing not only pictures of the severed leg, but actuarial charts that calculated the financial loss to the plaintiff over the remainder of their life."

Some of Walter's cases where various means of demonstrative evidence were used were:

1. **FIRST FEDERAL SAVING & LOAN v. WYLIE**, FL 1950, where anatomical charts were used to better understand the testimony of a medical doctor;

2. **ALLEN v. ST. LOUIS PUBLIC SVC**, MO 1956, where the doctor and technician who took x-rays interpreted the x-ray pictures;

3. **HAMPTON v. RUTENSTRAUCH**, MO 1960, where an entire skeleton, collars, braces, and traction devices were introduced showing the nature and extent of injuries;

4. **BOEING AIRPLANE CO v. BROWN**, 9 Cir. 1961, photographs were admitted into evidence under the "feasibility" doctrine. This was necessary because the defendant denied there was anything he could do to make the premises or condition more safe, or it was unreasonable to expect him to have done anything more. (Generally speaking, photographs are admissible in the case of damages, even though they may be gruesome as they go to the issue of pain and suffering.);

5. **CALANDRI v. IONE SCHOOL**, CA, 1963, another case where colored slides were admitted, showing the mashed condition of a child's hand;

6. **STREIT v. KESTEL**, OH, 1959, where experiments were permissible that recreated automobile skidding and speeding tests similar to those in the actual accident.

In all such cases, Walter Beckham said, "The proper rule toward permitting the introduction and use of demonstrative evidence should be to assist the jury in…determining the facts. The sound discretion of the trial judge is the guard against abuse…A proper picture or other visual demonstration is indeed worth a thousand words." Today, demonstrative evidence is commonplace in all courtrooms across the nation, and indeed, around the world. Walter and Perry were true pioneers in their field.

Courtroom 6-1, Dade County Courthouse, Miami, Florida

One rather famous place where Walter plied his trade was courtroom 6-1, located on the sixth floor of the Dade County Courthouse in downtown Miami. The courthouse was originally built during 1925-28, and a three-year restoration of courtroom 6-1 was completed in 2010. It remains the largest and most spectacular courtroom in the courthouse measuring fifty-eight feet, three inches long, thirty-four feet, four inches wide, floor to wood beams thirteen feet, three inches, and floor to ceiling fifteen feet, ten inches. The large ornately carved dark mahogany stained wooden beams, which support the ceiling, dominate the room. The walls knockdown plaster are painted off-white, which displays wonderful small shadows on its surfaces. The four large, floor-to-ceiling windows on the north side provide the only outside light. The judge's desk, the railings around the jury box and in front of the gallery church pew benches, are all heavy, bold, dark mahogany wood which complements the wooden beams above. Exact reproductions of the wall fans and seven light candelabras appear on the walls around the working end of the room. Beautiful brass, double-domed table lamp reproductions are set in front of and on each side of the judge's desk near the court reporter's desk. A present-day air-conditioning system is cleverly hidden behind five wooden lattice grills located high on the wall behind the judge's desk.

From 1928-1962, when courtroom 6-1 was designated the criminal court of record, nearly every felony case was tried there. Some of the most famous trials held there were:

- **1930**—While staying in his winter home on Palm Island, Miami Beach, across the bay from Miami, Al "Scarface" Capone was tried for perjury in what was then identified as courtroom 630. He "beat the rap" and returned to Chicago, only to be tried and convicted of tax evasion years later.

- **February 1933**—Guiseppe Zangara attempted to assassinate President-Elect Franklin D. Roosevelt on the porch of a hotel fronting on Biscayne Bay in Miami. He missed Roosevelt, but hit Chicago Mayor Anton Cermak, who was standing next to Roosevelt. Zangara pled guilty to four counts of attempted murder, and Judge E. C. Collins sentenced him to eighty years. Within days, Mayor Cermak died. Zangara pled guilty to murder and Judge Uly Thompson had him executed ten days later.

- **1935**—Judge Collins was tried for embezzlement and bribery. The jury was deadlocked, and Collins resigned the next day.

- **1966**—Socialite Candace "Candy" Mossler and her nephew/lover were tried for killing Mossler's wealthy husband, Jacques Mossler, in his Key Biscayne condo. The testimony was so salacious spectators under age twenty-one were not permitted in the courtroom. Both defendants were acquitted, though the police detectives continue to believe they were guilty.

- **1990s**—America's landmark tobacco trial between the four largest U.S. tobacco companies (Philip Morris, R. J. Reynolds, Brown & Williamson, and Lorillard) and the attorneys general of forty-six states was finally settled for over $200 billion.

Even with a very busy schedule, Walter shifted gears and found time to obtain a juris doctor (JD) degree in 1969, which further enhanced his pedigree. Walter also returned to teaching at UM that year, where he taught trial advocacy, torts, and medical-legal trial tactics until his retirement in 1982 as professor emeritus. While at UM he founded the first national Medical Institute for Attorneys and served as its director for fifteen years.

Walter never stopped paying back to the profession that gave him such success in life. In 1964, feeling he now had sufficient funds to repay his law school scholarship fund, he contacted the assistant dean of Harvard Law School, inquiring as to how much it would take to reimburse the school. He wanted to give back in memory of his father and to, in his words, "help the next guy." Assistant Dean Wesley E. Bevins Jr. dutifully reviewed the 1946-49 academic years, which indicated $175 came from the John Foster Fund, created in 1840, and $700 from the James A. Rumrill Fund, created in 1909, for a grand total of $875. Costs for everything were quite different then than now. Walter gladly and proudly remitted a check in the full amount by return mail.

The sheer magnitude of Walter's accomplishments both in the legal and private communities is overwhelming, but is most deserving of full recognition. During the ensuing years Walter's accomplishments included:

- Founding member of the initial 151-member The Florida Bar Association

- Founder of the National Institute of Trial Advocacy

- Founding member of the Academy of Florida Trial Lawyers Robert Orseck Building

- Member of United States Supreme Court

- Member of District of Columbia Bar

- Past president of the Junior Bar Section, Dade County Bar Association

- President of the Greater Miami YMCA

- Past member of Board of Governors, Junior Bar Section of The Florida Bar

- Past member Board of Directors and Executive Committee, Dade County Bar Association

- National vice chairman of Membership Committee, Insurance, Negligence and Compensation Section, American Bar Association (ABA)

- Member of ABA Special Commissions on Tort Liability System, and Association Governance

- Member of American Bar Foundation

- Member of the American College of Trial Lawyers

- Chairman of National Institute for Trial Advocacy

- Member of Inner Circle of Advocates

- Member of the Medical Institute for Attorneys

- Director of University of Miami School of Law

- Founding member of National Board of Trial Advocacy, Trustee and Chair Emeritus of National Judicial College

- Vice chairman, Aviation Section, American Trial Lawyers Association

- Member, American Trial Lawyers Association

- Member, Dade County Bar

- Member, American Bar Association

- President and member, International Academy of Trial Lawyers

- Member, International Academy of Law & Science

- Member, Law-Science Academy of America

- Member, Maritime Law Association of the United States

- Member, National Council of the YMCA

- Member Board of Directors, Dade County Crippled Children's Society

- Member, Kiwanis Club of Miami

- President, Century Club of Miami

- Recipient of the Academy of Florida Trial Lawyers Perry Nichols Award

- Recipient of the Emory University Medal

- Member of Dade County Mental Health Board

- Member of first class of YMCA Blue Ridge Assembly Board of Trustees

- Past chairman and member, Phi Alpha Delta Legal Fraternity

- First non-judge to become chairman of the Board of Trustees at the National Judicial College;

…and, lastly, he spearheaded the building of the sanctuary of the First United Methodist Church in Coral Gables, where his funeral service was later held. Serving actively and effectively in all these organizations was a feat unattainable by any lawyer save one, Walter Beckham, who did it with aplomb and respect by his peers for many, many years. He was a giant among men.

Daughter Barbara says, "Daddy (later Dad) was a stern and firm disciplinarian. Lying or stealing were the worst mistakes one could make." When she cheated on a third grade test she felt bad when confronted by her father. Chastising her he said, "Cheating is stealing other people's ideas." He also made her confess the crime to her teacher, which was very embarrassing. But she never made that mistake again. She also observed, "Dad did have a temper, but only scolded me, maybe because I was a girl." His temper must have been more recognized by her brothers. In high school, Barbara was not allowed to have a car, though some of her friends did. Walter explained she didn't need a car because he continued to drive his kids to school, though that practice ended during their high school years. In her last two years in high school, Walter encouraged her to consider becoming a lawyer, following in the generations of Beckham lawyers. He even had her work part-time in his office, hoping she would become attracted to the field of law. Though dutifully impressed with all the books, special thirteen-inch long yellow-lined tablets designed especially for lawyers, and the vernacular lawyers used when speaking to each other, Barbara decided the legal profession was not for her. Instead, she went in another direction and became a psychologist. She facetiously delighted in telling Walter she did it "to help repair all the damage lawyers do to people." Walter never quite accepted the dig on his profession, but she was a girl, and he would make his pitch to her brothers as they followed her in school. This was when Barbara first really saw the LOOK, when her dad got mad. She was no longer to be treated as a little girl. She was a young lady, and needed to act and be treated as such. Walter's stare, which was achieved by tilting his head down while looking over his glasses slipped down on his nose pince-nez style, resembled Queen Elizabeth's expression of disapproval, without uttering a word. He didn't need to say anything; his look showed disappointment in you for whatever the reason. This expression continued throughout his life, including when practicing law. He was saying without speaking, "I believe you are capable of doing better." Recipients felt they had let him down; thinking about the incident long after having left his presence.

Ever mindful of his point's requirements in the Naval Reserve in 1950, Walter spent his two weeks in summer training working at the Navy Ship's Store Office at the Brooklyn Navy Yard in New York. 1951, the year his third and last child, James "Jimmy," was born, found him at the Naval Gun Factory in Washington, DC, and in 1954, the year he was promoted to commander, he served aboard the USS *Champlain*, sailing out of Norfolk, Virginia. In 1956, he had a very special two-week summer training at the Naval Air Station, Key West. What made it so special was that he brought his family with him. They all had a great time on the beach and visiting the famous town. They visited Ernest Hemingway's home, had lunch at Sloppy Joes, watched sunsets on the dock, and did all the tourist things visitors do in Key West. The year 1958 saw him spend two

Commander Beckham, 1956

weeks with the Charleston Group, Atlantic Reserve Fleet at the U.S. Naval Base, Charleston, S.C. During these years he got to see a lot of places and ships at the expense of the Navy. Walter so loved to travel, seeing people, places, and things in far distant lands. To him, travel was another education available to those who chose to take advantage of it.

A few years later, summer training was a bit of a mystery. Walter took a special extension course from the Navy War College. The course was titled "Solution to Installment Six Extension Course in International Law." Was it a classified subject? He never said, but he took this course very seriously as it was one of the conditional requirements to being qualified for promotion to captain. It consumed one entire week of his waking hours. He immersed himself in the course as he did every legal case he ever tried. Walter III had never seen his dad so consumed by any project; and when he completed it, though asked what it was about, he never told young Walter or anyone else. He obviously completed the course with high marks, as he was promoted to captain, July 1, 1960.

These were also the years Walter's intellect and wisdom would shine. He separated the wheat from the chafe. He was extremely circumspect when reviewing his cases. Oftentimes he would examine a case from the opposing side to determine its weaknesses and strengths, which enabled him to better represent his client(s) on the elements of the case(s). This tactic is used by the military as they prepare for battles. Maybe that's where Walter got the idea, in the Pacific long ago. You learn all you can about your enemy, including thinking like they do, in order to plan an attack to defeat them. Instinct told him when to jab and parry, and when to duck. He was known to speak slowly and softly, making those around him listen very carefully to his every word. He knew if he shouted and talked too fast, people would not listen as closely to him. As a trial lawyer he was swift as a cat; at times a bit like Andy Griffith's Ben Matlock, fooling opposing counsel into believing they had the upper hand, only to find he had just chopped them off at the knees. He never showed his sweat, and changed confrontation to a debate, which he won 95 percent of the time in approximately 200 trials, all but 5 percent of which were before a jury. This was a truly phenomenal rate of success in the litigation field of law. He believed a good lawyer must keep meticulous files and records of everything, because in law, one needs to refer to past information for years and years after the initial event. His meticulous record keeping served as a great source in helping this author write his biography, yet another trait of an astute and gifted lawyer.

Three trials and one petition before the Florida Supreme Court serve as good examples of his trial acumen utilizing new approaches, specifically demonstrative evidence, to plaintiff's rights in trial procedures. Though demonstrative evidence of charts and scales, pictures and actual models of, say, an injured body part was radical at that time, it is a basic procedure used in today's courts. Until then, most money, influence, and brain power had been on the side of defense, namely big business and insurance companies.

In her book, *Memories of a Trial Lawyer*, Francis Hutcheson Hare recalls what is best described as a medico-legal breakthrough in the "effective representation of personal injury plaintiffs," most ably demonstrated by a team of trial lawyers. Introduced first as "The Medicine Shows" at a seminar at Tulane University in New Orleans, the team of trial lawyers, including Walter Beckham, enlightened attendees as to how to straighten out defense-oriented doctors regarding the various traumas and treatment of those seriously injured in accidents. The belief was that compensation should be paid to the plaintiff proportionate to his or her pain and suffering when recovering from what were often identified as life-altering injuries. Until then, many lawyers, judges, and juries were uneducated in the subject matter; they were just guided in medical issues by the physicians brought before them to testify. The initial seminar was so successful, Walter and his team took the show on the road, across the country, educating litigation lawyers on how to deal with doctors on a level playing field. Trial lawyers could then appear in court with essentially as much medical knowledge as the doctors on the witness stand.

The *Braddock v. Seaboard Air Line Railroad Company* case, and the two additional cases described below, were some of the first cases where individual rights won over the roughshod tactics of big businesses. In Braddock, two suits by a father and son arose out of a railroad crossing accident where a child's leg was amputated. Beckham successfully established that a plaintiff's counsel could make a *per diem* argument to the jury for pain and suffering damages, and that the award of damages for future pain and suffering was not subject to reduction to its present value.

In *Ratner v. Arrington*, Beckham established that a plaintiff's counsel could give suggested amounts to the jury in itemizing future damages, and that he could also use a blackboard/chart to display the itemization in closing argument.

The *Ford Motor Company v. Hill* case involved injuries by a passenger in a car owned and driven by another person. Beckham successfully established that the crash worthiness doctrine applied in strict liability cases.

Last, in 1968, Beckham petitioned the Florida Supreme Court, and won, allowing the University of Miami Law School to offer the state's first trial practice program, and to not have to run the risk of having the students' participation violate the state's Canons of Ethics. The Integration Rule of The Florida Bar was dutifully amended by adding to Article XVIII the designation "Law School Civil Practice Program," which meant "any law student in an accredited Florida law school may gratuitously assume the role of an advocate in a law school-sponsored trial practice program directly supervised by a lawyer licensed to practice in Florida, and involving insured non-personal injury claims only, wherein the rights of the claimants will be finally determined pursuant to the voluntary submission and agreement of all parties in interest." These were hard-fought battles that directly impacted how plaintiff cases would be tried from those days forward.

While active in the ABA, Walter fought for maintaining a jury system, maintaining the tort liability system, maintaining punitive damages, preventing the federalization of the products liability and medical malpractice systems, preventing the adoption at both the state and federal levels of an automobile no-fault system, and was the force behind the "Beckham Amendment," by which sections of the Bar forged a more equitable sharing in the governance of the ABA. Probably the most widely recognized effort of Walter's by the general public, occurred at the 1989 ABA annual meeting in Honolulu, Hawaii. The hot topic was whether burning the American flag was or should be legal. People all over the city, including cab drivers, were tuned in to hear the discussion. Walter, ever the eloquent speaker he was, made an impassioned speech before the House of Delegates against making it legal to burn the American flag, telling of the enormous importance the flag has been and forever will be to our military troops, particularly during time of war. Walter III was at the meeting where his dad made him feel so proud to be an American. During the duration of the meeting, young Walter watched as his father moved from place to place at the meeting, frequently followed by an entourage. Lawyers wanted to be around Walter, recognizing the wisdom in his reasoning, speech, and writing acumen. Walter was at the top of his game, jousting with the best in the business, giving no quarter, and winning most of the time. He justifiably earned every accolade ever bestowed on him.

Many years later, Walter reflected on his years of being an active trial lawyer, comparing a trial lawyer to a prize fighter, telling Walter III the intellectual and emotional blows taken in the courtroom are not unlike that of a prize fighter in the ring. The effects are cumulative like a head concussion, and eventually take their toll on one. Trial lawyers, like professional athletes, have a limited career span, where age, strength, agility, and expertise decline. One must know when to hang up the gloves. Those who stay in the ring too long get knocked out. The aging trial lawyer will eventually end up either one of the "a'holics" (alcohol, sex, or drugs), or alone because of anger and continually having to suppress one's emotions. Walter recognized the time and moved on. Later that year he became of counsel to the highly successful trial and appellate litigation firm of Podhurst & Orseck, P.A. Today the firm continues to be extremely successful and enjoys a well-deserved stellar reputation as one of the finest litigation law firms in the country.

A GRANDSON'S LOVE

Following in the footsteps of several generations of Beckham attorneys, it is no surprise Walter's grandson, Justin Beckham, Jimmy's son, is now practicing law in his own firm, DeFabio, Beckham and Solis, in Miami. Justin has fond memories of his grandfather that are best remembered in his own words. One can feel the love he had, and has, of his late grandfather:

"My grandfather told me when he was growing up that his father (my great-grandfather) was the best student in his school. He was also the fastest runner, the best wrestler, the best at everything. My grandfather often wondered how this was possible, presumably pressuring himself to be the same as a young boy. One day, my great-grandfather told my grandfather there was one small detail he left out of his childhood story after all these years, and that was his entire school class only consisted of eight people.

When I was eight years old my grandfather told me if I memorized the entire list of U.S. presidents in order and could recite the list in front of him, he would give me a gift. I practiced every day and finally gave him my rendition, which I still remember to this day. His gift was a book filled with 50 silver coins, each representing a different state. Memorizing that list helped me in so many unexpected ways during my academic career.

My grandfather loved Emory. He used to wrestle in college, and for lunch he would often just have a Coca Cola, a piece of chocolate and peanut butter on crackers, in order to make weight. My grandfather also loved the University of Miami, and donated the mace they still use in the graduation ceremony. He always watched the Hurricane football games. He also loved to swim in the ocean off Key Biscayne.

He loved hunting, giving me a shotgun when I turned 12 years old. One day I decided to eat a fireball candy and drink orange juice for breakfast while at our hunting camp. I rode on the truck and threw up. Grandfather walked with me next to the truck for awhile until I felt better. He often said to walk in the shade when you can, because there will come a day when there is no shade. He believed 'sweet are the lessons of adversity.'

We had family dinner together almost every Sunday night when he and grandmother were in town. It was special when they, my parents, my sister, and I all went to Tony Romas. I always looked forward to when grandfather would return from a trip, because he would bring us coins from every different country he had visited. Coins were always a nice treat.

Speaking of wrestling, I was so very happy when my grandfather watched me win the District Wrestling Championship at my high school. He was often in the crowd for as many of my sporting events he could attend, which I truly appreciated.

I remember people would walk up to my grandfather regularly at airports, or restaurants, and always say how he was their inspiration to becoming a lawyer, or how they would always remember his class at the law school.

When he visited me at school in San Francisco, he took me out for a drink and meal at a fancy restaurant, and told me he fondly remembered calling my grandmother from San Francisco when he returned from the war, telling her he was finally coming home.

One time my grandfather, my dad and I were in Uncle Walter's house, waiting for him to come home from a very important trial. When Uncle Walter returned with the very good news, grandfather said 'you made your living.' This was a very special moment for us all. He always told me this was my job in life, to make a living for my family. He was an amazing grandfather in every sense of the word, and an amazing person to know and look to for advice. I will forever love him."

Walter's oldest son, Walter III, was young when the family first moved to Coral Gables. But he remembers their little house on Zamora Avenue. It was near an airport, a drive-in theater, and a dog track. The house had three bedrooms and one bathroom. In 1956, they sold the house for $15,500 and moved to a bigger house on Santa Maria Street, near the Riviera Country Club. The backyard was full of avocado, guava, lime, lemon, and cherry trees, the fruits from which Ethel prepared and served on the dining room table. Walter didn't play golf at Riviera, but he played a lot of tennis, and won frequently. He was a club member for business purposes. Many legal agreements were often crafted at the club before being submitted to the court.

Walter III also remembers "Old Man Pop" with heartfelt fondness and respect, though somewhat differently than Barbara. His big sister never received an allowance, because being a girl, she wasn't assigned any chores around the house. First, young Walter received a weekly allowance of $2.50, but when he entered high school, his allowance increased to $5.00 a week for washing the family cars and sweeping the patio. He said Pop (later Dad) would pick and choose his battles, finding him to be strict, firm, and difficult to deal with. He firmly believes WWII changed his father, who seemed to have a short fuse, causing one to walk on egg shells, for fear Pop would all of a sudden go off like a cherry bomb fire cracker.

Jimmy, the maverick of Walter's children, tells yet a different story. He remembers Dad as being extremely busy, not having time to play ball in the backyard, which disappointed Jimmy greatly. On the all-too-often occasions of Jimmy misbehaving, Ethel told him "wait until your father gets home." On these occasions of serious issues, Walter did not scold Jimmy in the house. Rather, he took him to his office at the University of Miami. In his law office, Walter was judge and jury. Punishment would come in the form of a whipping with a leather brush. Walter had a strict father, and he was fully prepared to be the same when the situation called for it. Other, less serious punishment, often meant Jimmy was assigned additional chores around the house, such as cleaning up the garage.

Fonder memories were the generous vacations, such as cruises in the Caribbean and a trip to the Grand Canyon. In the 1960s, Jimmy became a hippy with long hair and a beard. One time, Jimmy was drunk at a Coral Gables high school football game, and decided to have some fun running alongside a moving car, falling, and skinning himself severely on the asphalt road. He made it home and told his dad he was hurt. Walter quickly took him to the hospital emergency room where Jimmy was treated and released. Walter never said a word about the drunken incident. What would have been the purpose? It was done; Jimmy had hurt himself, and would most likely learn from the incident. Nothing Walter could have said would have changed anything. By the time Jimmy turned nineteen, he had been dating his girlfriend, Thorne, since eighth grade. Though his mom had encouraged him to date other girls, her advice didn't carry much weight, as she had never dated anyone other than

Walter since junior high. When Jimmy told Walter he and Thorne were going to get married later that year, Walter emphatically told him he was much too young. Asking if Jimmy had a plan, Jimmy told him no. But Walter did help with their wedding, and of course, has helped Jimmy and Thorne the same as his other children ever since. They were family. In college, Jimmy was again caught drinking and went before the school's honor counsel, and received only a warning. Walter felt a need to keep Jimmy busy, and to help him earn some money, since he had a family to support while still in college. Walter got Jimmy a summer job in a factory that made truck parts. It was honest labor, which Walter believed would help Jimmy prepare for life after college.

Three or four times a year during their secondary school years, Walter would take young Walter and Jimmy hunting in the Nichols hunting camp, which was about 15,000 acres of land on the Curly Wolf Ranch near Altamonte Springs on the west coast of Florida. When Jimmy turned twelve or thirteen, he got his first shotgun. The hunting cabin in the Nichols hunting camp had no electricity and an outhouse instead of a bathroom. For a boy who had grown up with electric lights, air conditioning, and a bathroom with a toilet and shower, this was a little too much roughing it for Jimmy's taste, though young Walter seemed to love it. Jimmy more enjoyed fishing from a boat on the Gulf of Mexico. While the boys learned to hunt deer, quail, and wild turkey, they were also responsible for taking care of the guns and Jeep. Little did they know the experience would serve them well a few years later.

Soon after, the time had come for Walter and Ethel to introduce their beautiful daughter, Barbara, to Coral Gables society. The year was 1963. First there was a dinner dance at the Kings Bay Yacht and Country Club, where Barbara wore a gorgeous yellow dress with green trim. Next came the Debutante Ball, held at the Surf Club, where she wore a beautiful white floor-length dress. All of society was there, and it was expensive. Walter was busting his buttons with pride. Barbara was statuesque in her long white dress. All the men took note and were very envious of her two, not one, but two escorts, Heath Allen and John Nichols (son of Walter's partner Perry Nichols). Barbara had arrived. This was her day, and there was a big article in the *Miami Herald* newspaper commemorating the event.

Walter and Ethel at Barbara's Debutante Ball

Young Walter and Jimmy were not so impressed. Not long after Barbara's Debutante Ball was over, they approached dad and asked inquiringly and respectfully, "What do guys get?" Walter pondered the question for a bit, then asked them what did they think would be equal to the Ball and appropriate for them? Walter III was quick to respond, "How about taking me and Jimmy hunting in Africa? Perry Nichols took his kids there."

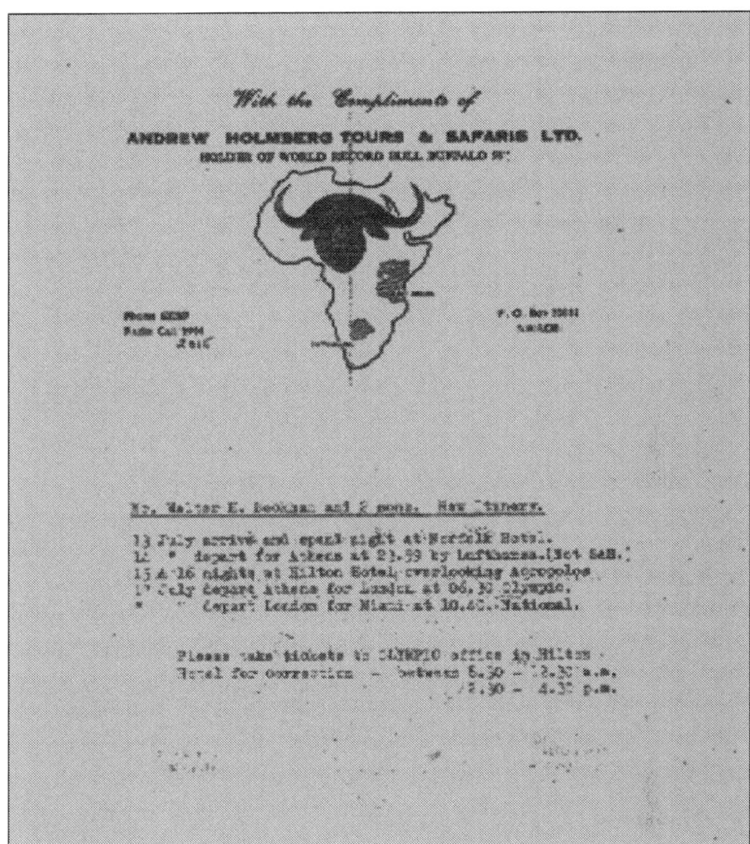

HUNTING IN EAST AFRICA

Walter said okay, as the cost was somewhat equivalent to the cost of their sister's Ball. They were to be gone five weeks. Walter hired Andrew Holmberg, the most famous white hunter in Kenya of all time, and godson to Karen Blixen (author of *Out of Africa*). Andrew was actually born in the Blixen's home, and later learned his trade from Karen's husband and second cousin, Baron Bror von Blixen-Finecke. Andrew earned his fame measured by the inches and pounds of ivory he took down over the years, which far exceeds that of any other white hunter. Now in his 90s, Andrew intends to sell or donate his trophies to museums around the world, to be viewed by millions of people for many years to come.

Walter, young Walter, and Jimmy left Miami for Nairobi, Kenya on June 10, 1963, carrying five guns and ammunition. Walter had researched the type of guns they would need, so he carried a Winchester .300 H&H magnum rifle, Jimmy a Seiko .300 magnum rifle, and Walter III had a Weatherby .300 magnum rifle—all using 250 grain ammunition designed for all the game they were to hunt save the huge elephants, rhinoceros, and Cape buffalo. For those, the white hunter would provide much bigger guns.

Kenya was a country still in the throes of gaining independence from the British Empire. It had just experienced a four-year-long uprising by Jomo Kenyatta's Mau Maus, who terrorized the country raiding towns and villages, indiscriminately brutalizing and killing people, and burning homes and buildings in their path. Kenyatta had long been the leader of the secret Kikuyu Central Association, which sought African representation in the government. The British forces finally put down the violence, which saw 100 whites killed, 200 Kikuyu who did not support the movement killed, and 11,000 Mau Maus killed. But the cause was a success. In 1960, while Kenyatta was still in prison, he was elected president of the new Kenya African National Union, which was given a majority of seats in the government. A year later he was released from prison, and in 1963 he became prime minister of the newly independent Republic of Kenya.

Andrew reserved two blocks of land consisting of 500 square miles in the Rift Valley, some 180 miles due north of Nairobi, on which they were licensed to hunt for five weeks. The licenses cost $500 each, and the same amount was then charged for each animal they shot. Big game hunting in Africa was expensive. But since game had not been hunted in this area for fifteen years, the game were expected to be big and plentiful.

Upon arrival in Nairobi, and meeting Andrew for the first time, the first hitch in their great adventure erupted. Andy typically hunted with no more than two hunters, and they numbered three. So he independently hired another white hunter for the third hunter. And, of course, he wanted more money for the second white hunter, which raised the price from $318 per day to $390 per day. Walter was furious. He was not about to pay one dollar more than the contracted price.

Walter, Walter III, and Jimmy heading out

After about ten or fifteen minutes of very animated discussion, where Walter used his exceptional negotiating powers of reasoning and compromise learned in years spent in the courtrooms of America, the trip was reduced to four weeks, and they were set to head into the bush. Young Walter would initially go with Andrew on one block, and Walter and Jimmy would hunt with Pete Smith, another white hunter, in another block. At some point later, they would switch hunters according to Andrew's direction. They would travel roughly twenty miles each day on camel and horseback, setting up fly camps each night. The system used was to track and stalk on foot, zebra, kudu, élan, dik dik, lion, Cape buffalo, impala, elephant, and leopard. The daily routine was grueling as they left early in the morning, often not returning to camp until after dark. The hunters typically arose around 4:30 a.m. and received information from the scouts at breakfast as to where the game had been sighted. These scouts would number anywhere from one to three. Their job was to go out ahead of the hunting parties one to three days earlier. Each team of hunters had a specific line of march designed with safety and secrecy in mind. One cannot easily sneak up on the game, for the game have very, very sensitive senses designed to protect them from any animal or person bent on doing them harm. In the lead of each team was a tracker, followed by a game scout who carried a lightweight wooden tripod for spur of the moment standing shots. Next came one of the Beckhams, followed by a white hunter. A couple of game skinners brought up the rear. But that was just the hunting parties. In addition, there were cooks, horse and camel handlers, and several "gophers" available to help in any function needed. Clothing for the Beckhams consisted of tan ankle-high "desert boots," long-sleeve and long-legged cotton khaki shirts and pants, and a khaki jacket with four patch pockets. And, of course, they each donned an obligatory wide-brim bush hat. A friend of Walter III lent him a pair of 10-power Zeiss binoculars, which proved to be of inestimable value when searching the distant terrain for game. They each had a camera, but didn't take many photos. Their minds were set on shooting game with their rifles, not their cameras. Dawn and dusk were the best times to hunt, as that was when the game was most active and feeding. Sometimes the hunters would hang bait from a tree in the form of a gazelle or hind quarter of a zebra, shot by Walter, Walter III, or Jimmy. When bait was used, the hunters would have to sneak into their blinds near the bait and wait, in hopes of getting a clean shot. Sometimes the game wasn't large enough and Andrew or Peter would make the call to let it go. Let it grow so that next time you might get a trophy head, they would say. Trust in the skills of Andrew and Peter were truly tested when stalking lions. They crawled on their bellies through high grass, unable to see more than a few yards ahead, worrying they might come face to face with a lion. They also had to wonder how Andrew and Peter could see the lions out a hundred or more yards where they could take a shot, sometimes using a Y-shaped aiming stake to rest their gun on. Of all the trophies and skins they brought back of zebras, kudus, impalas, elands, Cape buffalo, Thomson's gazelles, leopards, elephants, and rhinoceros, two kills were most memorable, one by young Walter and one by Jimmy. Each involved personal danger. At the time, it was not unheard of for a wild animal to attack and kill a hunter. This was not a game they were playing in the bush of East Africa. This was a life or death experience that would stay with them for the rest of their lives.

One day, young Walter saw a Cape buffalo sleeping. Andrew gave the three-stick sign, raising and lowering his walking stick three times meaning "it's show time." The buffalo, awakened by their presence, charged them through the thick brush. The Cape buffalo is only about five feet tall, but it has huge horns and weighs in at about 2,600 pounds. That is one formidable sight when it is running toward you and it's mad at you. Walter fired, reloaded, and fired three times into the heart, but the buffalo didn't go down. Finally, when it was dangerously close, about five yards away, Andrew helped him bring the beast down with one shot to the heart. All of young Walter's other kills were clean, one shots, sometimes at distances of 200 or more yards, but they paled by comparison to this exciting episode. Walter III was an exceptionally good shot from great distances. He would have been a good Marine sniper, had he chosen to join the Corps.

Jimmy, on the other hand, had an even scarier experience. He recalls they had nineteen gun and supply bearers along with the camels and horses they rode to get into the bush block. On his famous day, Jimmy spotted a leopard in a tree with the hind leg of a zebra in its jaws. Taking his shot, Jimmy landed one shot in the leopard's chest that made it mad. It dropped out of sight into a lair in a pile of huge boulders. It could leap out from any direction. The gun bearers fired crossfires in an attempt to flush the leopard out. Then suddenly the leopard leaped out, heading for the gun bearers, mauling one of them before Pete could reach over and shoot it off. Pete fired and missed as Jimmy and the gun bearers all fired and missed. With the leopard about to pounce on Jimmy, Pete fired again, this time hitting the leopard in the heart and killing it. Five seconds later and Jimmy would have been lunchmeat for the leopard. When the hunt ended, all the trophies and skins were shared in Walter's, young Walter's, Jimmy's, and friends' houses. Walter gave a full Grevy's zebra skin to Carole, his law firm administrator. (Carole and I married many years later, and the zebra skin has graced our bedroom floor ever since. We cannot look at it without thinking of Walter, a true friend). The Grevy's zebra, which is located in the northern mountain and coastal areas of Kenya, is named after

Jules Grevy, president of France in 1880, who was given one as a gift. They are taller and heavier, somewhat like a horse, with a big head and ears. Their stripes are numerous, but do not cover their belly. The Burchell zebra, known as the common zebra, is smaller than the Grevy, has stripes that stretch all the way around their bodies, and are most common in the savannah and plains of Kenya and Tanzania.

Both Walter and young Walter kept meticulous daily diaries of their hunt. Walter's was only recently found by his son, Walter, in 2012. While hunting in the mountains and savannahs of East Africa, it is most intriguing to read his thoughts of the hunt, and that of his time in the South Pacific some twenty years before.

Excerpts from Walter's Diary...

"Left Miami today. Ethel took us to the plane. The Captain let us put our guns (three .300 Winchester Magnum rifles, three .375 Holland & Holland Magnum rifles and one 12 gauge shotgun) in the cabin to New York. Paid no excess baggage and carried our ammunition in shoulder-strap overnite bags. Boy, were they heavy…Had a good dinner, I took a sleeping pill and slept pretty well…Jimmy read his book "The Godfather," and Walter didn't get much sleep I'm afraid. He was too excited…saw all the tourist sites in Rome, St. Peter's Basilica, Victor Emmanuel memorial, The Pantheon, Vatican Museum was closed, Trevi Fountain, Forum, Coliseum, Via Veneto, and lunch at Wimpy's…before landing in Nairobi, we saw Mt. Kenya and Mt. Kilimanjaro from the air, also a vast countryside and a couple of big lakes…spent the day walking around Nairobi taking pictures of animal life, Nairobi University, Moslem Mosque, Statue to War Dead and our Hilton Hotel…posted letter to Ethel and cards to mother, Podhurst et al, Nichols et al, Bob Beckham and went to bed early…Andrew promised they would try to help us get all our trophies, and offered use of his lodge at times in exchange for the extra week…on the 2 ½ hour ride through the Rift Valley we saw our first zebra, Thomson's gazelle, and dik dik…took the boys picture right on the equator today…stopped for a view of Thompson's Falls

and the most beautiful mountain and plains scenery toward our base camp, along with large herds of zebra, Thomson's gazelle, élan, Grant's gazelle, and ostrich…Jimmy shot a nice Grant's gazelle buck for meat at about 150— 200 yards out with Pete's .375, a nice shoulder shot and we strapped it on the hood. This big plain is about 6,500 feet high, as we pass some Samburu villages with their cattle and children moving around their clay huts…had a good dinner of buffalo tongue and vegetables.

What's for dinner?

After each day's dinner, we all cleaned our guns in preparation for the next day's hunt. A lion, leopard and big elephant had all been near our camp last night and a leopard was working on bait we had out…we had gasoline lanterns and electric lights in our tents run on batteries. The night is quiet. I have a nice camp chair in my tent and a table and bed. Just heard something moving outside. I wonder, might it be a lion?

Samburu warriors with Walter's elephant

We get up at 6:20 in morning and after breakfast go to sight in our guns… each of us shot Pete's .465 elephant gun one time to get used to it. A very large bullet, a pretty good kick and lots of noise…got word from our spotters that there is leopard activity at two leopard baits so we will go leopard hunting on the horses after lunch. We have decided that Jimmy gets first shot at the leopard and I will sit in the leopard blind with Pete…examined some native spears today when two Samburu warriors painted with red dye on heads and shoulders visited our camp. The spears were very well made and very sharp with little leather scabbards over the spear edges. Had a dinner of Grant's gazelle, which was quite good. No animals shot today…Got out my New Testament from World War II this morning to read a few verses and saw what Ethel and mother and dad had written in it when I was off to war. This brought tears to my eyes…After breakfast I decided Walter would hunt alone with Andrew for awhile and Jimmy and I would go to fly camp with Pete. After saying goodbye to Walter and Andy, we set out on horseback about 11:30. Pete's trackers and skinner walking ahead and the horse trainer leading the procession on his horse. We rode and walked leading the horses for just over 2 hours in the very hottest part of the day. I walked most of the way as my backside is still getting used to the saddle… Saw a big herd of eland, it was decided I would try to shoot one and we stalked them for about an hour without getting a good shot…found a herd of about 40 elephants feeding.

They were all cows and calves as far as we could see and we stalked them about 45 minutes to try to see if a bull was around. Finally a cow saw our tracker and Pete and almost charged them. So we retreated to give it up… scouts are out but still no word on big game…Saw a congress of baboons of all sizes making their way to a mountaintop to spend the night on the rocks and trees there. They were very interesting as they talked back and forth. No shooting and back to camp for a cold beer, dinner, a shower and bed. Saw a big manyatta (Samburu home made of cow-dung clay) with lots of natives and spent some time watching them while Jimmy was hunting. All the little boys go naked and the women have a shawl-type covering that goes around them and leaves one breast exposed. The men wear a one-piece shawl also with sandals and a spear. They leave it split open on one side and tuck it under when they sit down. The women wear many strings of beads on their necks, arms and leg bracelets in profusion. Their main food is cow blood which is drained from the jugular vein without killing the cow, and mixed with cow milk. This food is high in protein. They eat very little meat. The milk containers are washed out and sterilized with cow urine which works very well due to its high ammonia content. I am told there is much congenital syphilis among these tribes on the northern frontier of Kenya…We will go back up to the big plain on John Dyke's place and hunt plain's game and also kill some zebra for lion and leopard bait…Jimmy is exhausted; he walked 10-15 miles in last three days…Have been hunting for 5 days and have shot 1 Grant's gazelle. Hope Walter is having good luck…It was a very bumpy 20-mile ride going up hill most of the way. About 0830 I shot a common zebra which our skinner skinned on the spot. Later in the morning Jimmy shot a nice onyx with 29-inch horns. Will make a beautiful full head mount…I missed two shots at Thomson's gazelle then shot a onyx with nice 27½ inch horns; A very pretty head. Jimmy missed a Thomson and we returned to camp…Watched the skinner skin the onyx and prepare our trophies. They will salt everything down tonight… The moon was gorgeous last night but is now on the wane and comes up later every night. The stars are gorgeous tonight. Just like I used to see in the South Pacific. The Southern Cross is visible here and was beautiful this am. Tracker told us he had found 5 bull elephants not far from camp and there is also a leopard which is bothering a village close by. Things are looking up. We had a big young bull elephant block the road on us for about 5 minutes on our way back to camp and staring hard and flopping his ears at us. We stopped, turned on the lights on the truck and watched as he finally moved on off and we proceeded. Quite a place…Got some scratches from some thorn trees which got infected from the water we wash in. Doctoring them with zinc oxide and band aids…Took a couple shots at some guinea fowl but they were out of range. Saw some gerenuk but not one that would make a good trophy. Saw four giraffe grazing. One of them was a huge fellow. They saw us and ran. The big fellow could have looked in a 5-story window. Saw two groups of elephants on the mountainside across the valley…Had onyx liver, delicious pineapple and banana for lunch…Jimmy shot a Grevy's zebra stallion which was very large. My horse was not feeling well so I had to walk about 2 miles back to camp at noon. Guess we saw 500 head of Samburu cattle down at the water with little boys driving the cattle… Later I shot an Impala which Pete estimated the tusks weighed 70-80 pounds. Very good eating…I took a shot at a big bull eland but hit him high on the shoulder and he ran off in high gear. Pete, John and I followed him about 3 miles and it was obvious we would never catch him so we gave up the chase…soaked an infected thumb from the thorn puncture and opened it up tonight. It is getting better…Had a letter from Walter waiting which was written yesterday. So far he has only shot an onyx and 2 Grant's gazelle which greatly surprised me…Up at 0500 and had breakfast of toast, coffee, marmalade, pineapple and oatmeal…Shot a big 2,000 pound eland with mange and a tapeworm, so did not keep the skin, but will keep his two tremendous front hoofs and one good horn to make bookends and a lamp. Jimmy shot a nice gerenuk which is strapped on the camel to take back to camp…Pete found a group of 3 bull elephants and said the biggest set of tusks were fairly long but slender and probably weighed about 40–45 pounds each. Jimmy set off with his .375 rifle, Pete with his .454 elephant gun, Labun with a .480 double barrel and Kimanierq with a .375 rifle. We heard 4 shots followed by more shots, the elephant then trumpeted, then one more shot and quiet. Jimmy will be happy with these tusks…We were mighty tired when we got in and drank water, coke and beer and soaked our feet in warm salt water which felt mighty good. I started taking declostatin for my infected hands and hope it will help clear it up…

Walter with elephant

Found Walter and Andrew had come into camp about midnight. Walter shot a lesser kudu, looked at several rhino and elephant but had not shot as Andrew didn't think they were huge enough…We decided we would go right home after our hunt rather than knock around Africa another week. So Judy (Andrew's wife) is to try and get our reservations changed. Also, I am going back with Andrew to try to get a big elephant while Walter and

Jimmy go with Pete for chances of getting lion and leopard…Andrew is very conscientious and spent a long time this morning explaining and showing me how to use the scope and tripod and how to shoot from various positions and the angles to shoot from depending on your relationship to the animal. The point of it all is to try to shoot right between the two front shoulders about 1/3 of the way up from the bottom of the body. This is where the heart and main arteries of all 4-legged game are located. Bandit trappers seem to have caught some lions and leopards with bear traps. The game rangers have killed several of them and found one group with 70 leopard skins. They evidently sell them in the Orient. As a result they have also just about killed off all the hyenas and all the remaining lion and leopard are very wary of approaching anything they don't kill themselves, namely our bait…The boys and I are getting lonesome for our girls and will be ready to leave at the end of our time. It is a rare experience to see and be around all these animals roaming in their native habitat, and to see the Samburu settlements with thorn fences around them where man and his cattle have learned to live compatibly to a large extent with their environment without changing it at all for thousands of years. This is completely unspoiled here and not very many white men have ever really been to this remote spot."

Excerpts from Walter III's Diary...

"Dad said he had seen in the Nairobi paper that Andrew's sister had died so we figured we will start the safari a bit late…Awoke to "tea buana" at 6:30. (Buana means Earth, but in East Africa at the time it meant white man or boss.)…We crossed the equator at about 11:00 and it was really a neat feeling. It is hard to think that I am really below the equator for the first time and that we are on the continent of Africa…Took a few pictures at Thompson's Falls… Since we needed camp meat, Pete took Jimmy to shoot a Grant's gazelle on the plain. Jimmy took two sitting shots at a tremendously far range and missed both with his .300 magnum. After traveling a bit more, Jimmy took another shot with Pete's .357 while resting on the back of the jeep and made a perfect shot…Andrew awakened Pop at 5:55 p.m. telling him that SIMBA

(lion) had been feeding on our bait and that a hunt was ready to begin. Since Jimmy had hunted the leopard bait the night before, I was elected, dressed and shoved off about 6:15. Rode horses with Pete Smith about ½ hour out of camp, dismounted on edge of a gully 2 ridges over from camp and walked to the blind about 40 yards from the zebra bait…Rode on in the rain until we saw a group of Grant's gazelles. Rode to a vacant covered hut, jumped out and prepared to shoot. Rested on a railing about waist high, as the position was awkward as neither knee was touching the ground for support. At about 125 yards I shot a bit high and hit the neck just above the spine. Grant was stunned but walked a bit and stopped, shot in same position high again and missed. Grant ran about 150 yards and stopped again. Andrew told me to stand up and rest on a 2X4 running horizontal to the rail. Standing shot with left hand rest was good and dropped Grant with perfect heart shot… Andrew gave me pointers on my shooting. Told me to use 2 or 3 power scope magnification instead of 5 or 6, because the high magnification produces too many movements while aiming…Saw Grant's gazelle, tried a standing shot with prop at about 350 yards. Andrew told me to aim at the center and I missed. Didn't think we allowed enough for drop. Andrew agreed. Saw another about a half mile away, and after walking to within about 250 yards I again sat on a termite hill and propped against the right leg. Gazelle was 45 degree going away and feeding when I shot it right down. Walked it off and distance was 264 yards. Shot went through the back leg facing me, and entered the chest right in the middle of the body…We saw a huge elephant in the road with about 55–60 pound tusks. What a tremendous animal. We let it wander in the headlights until it wandered off the road as we didn't know what it might do…Had a scotch before dinner of soup, buffalo steak, mashed potatoes, whole carrots and pineapple and bananas for dessert…Sun began to break just 10 minutes later and we rode until 6:15 a.m. Stopped the horses a good 200 yards behind where we had left them yesterday and walked in with the two trackers. The two gun bearers stayed behind. Arrived in blind at 6:25 and waited five minutes if that. A female leopard was feeding on the bait so we left. Back in the gully Andrew pointed out the congress of baboons on top of the big rocks above the area we had hunted. I thought they were buzzards until I watched them through field glasses. What a zoo. Made me think of

Howie (girlfriend) and our two trips to the Atlanta Zoo. I really miss her and await anxiously my return to Atlanta. Saw four large elephant tracks on the way back and sent two trackers to look them over…Woke up at 10:30 because about 10 flies were about to carry me out of bed. They are a nuisance, but twice as good as mosquitoes. Finally found out what that awful smell is that seems to be everywhere…These large ants secrete it as a defensive measure, and they are everywhere as are the flies. Liver again for lunch, so I had no meat except a sausage. First time we have had it and it was quite good. French avocado and mango for dessert before Andrew and I left at 1:00 for block 54-A…On the way we saw 2 Grevy's zebra and 3 or 4 bunches of giraffe. They are called reticulated giraffe, and are supposed to be the most beautiful. Also saw many large trees uprooted with large limbs torn down by the elephants. Looked like they had been hit by a hurricane. Camp is on the bank of about a 40-yard wide dried up stream bed. Our water hole is dug in the center and is at least 12 feet deep where there is a small pool of water. There are about 25 camels here, the larger being twice the size of our horses. We will sleep in sleeping bags under mosquito nets as the breeze is brisk and feels good…Had quite a sinking feeling all day as hunting by yourself is quite lonesome as you have no one to really talk with or anyone to share with when you make a good shot or down a fine trophy. I will be glad when I join Dad next half of the hunt as I want him to shoot a big elephant more than I want any of my trophies. Hope he can shoot his small stuff with Pete and come over here and concentrate on bagging a big one…Awake at 5:30, can't help but think back to Spring Quarter when I was getting up at 10:00 or 11:00. Wish I was still going back to college again next year. Took the temperature of two of the men after breakfast. They could have malaria and one of the trackers seems to be having an asthma attack. Andrew plays doctor gives them both pills and tells them they will be well tomorrow. He only allows them one day for sickness…The trip today was about 15 to 18 miles. Andrew said we would have gone farther had we not had the two sick men. If we had gone farther, we probably would have had more than two. I know of a third. My backside is really sore from that saddle, and I am pretty tired. Saw a group of about 6 female and baby elephants, a few giraffe, a Grevy's zebra, and a few onyxes…Andrew noticed I was beginning to turn yellow from the alebrin taken every day for malaria. He suggested I not take one today and take darabrin tomorrow and only once a week from now on. He said there had been many cases of alebrin poisoning and that it eventually drives one crazy. Will start darabrin tomorrow and see what happens…It is too hot for a full beard, but I left a mustache to see how it will look. Figured Dad to do at least that, and the old man and Jimmy would give me hell if I didn't have some hair on my face. They are going to look like trolls when this thing is over and want me to also…This day was going to be different. The spotters heard lions playing. We just walked right into the brush. Saw some tracks of a male, female, and two cubs and began to follow. I couldn't believe we were actually tracking lions in such thick stuff. Around a bend we ran into a lesser kudu, with seven good sized impala. Got set on the tripod and almost shot the kudu, but it wasn't mature enough. One of the impala was real nice but Andrew didn't want to spook the lions. Saw a male impala and gerenuk about 10 feet away.

Walter with rhinoceros

By 9:00 it is so hot that most of the game have taken cover, so we mounted up and proceeded onward. Andrew told me we <u>must</u> have lion bait by today, so we do not return to camp for lunch…saw a cobra slither down a bush and into a hole in the ground about 5 feet away…Had two Grant's down by 2:00. The first shot was through the heart at about 65 yards and the second was about 3" high at about 100 yards. Though it went straight down it didn't kill it. Had to stick Andrew's knife into its brain and it made me sick. I really don't like killing these things at all because they are so tame, but Andrew wanted bait. After the necessary pictures, we perched them on camels and set out for the place where we had seen the lion. We ran into some Samburu warriors carrying some onyx meat. They said a lion had killed it and that some people from our camp had helped themselves to the meat. Andrew was furious. They had not only messed with the lion over bait, but also taken it away…Saw a beautiful fish eagle on the way back to camp. Had a white neck and tail with a jet black body, the most majestic bird I have ever seen… Andrew told me one of the horses was sick and lying down with a stomach ache. He took the kind of human stomach ache pills, dissolved them in a coke and gave it to the horse. Now it is up and eating again. Wonder what he will do to me if I get sick. Probably give me horse medicine. Good night…I am finally relaxing a bit and enjoying the hunting more as I have gotten to that point reached in football where the sore spots are laughable and you resign yourself to the fact that the going is always going to be hard so you begin to enjoy it for what it's worth. This is hard hunting, but the trophies are large and are satisfying when gotten…Arose at 3:50 as Andrew wanted me to sit around the fire with him and listen to the lions roar. Gradually they drifted eastward, so at 5:40 we set out on foot for bait…We stopped, for not 15 yards in front a lion was evidently stalking an eland, and caught our wind. He sprang to attention and shot through the tall grass and brush and was out of sight before a shot could be fired. We went straight out almost on a run and gave pursuit. Crouched and straining our eye and ears, we suddenly heard his paws hitting the sand around us and he seemed to be circling us. It was quite a feeling for a moment when I perceived the hunters were themselves being hunted. And the lion was gone…Jimmy had shot a 40 pound tusk elephant yesterday and since my main interest was lion and leopard, and further since

Dad had said more than once that he wanted a big elephant, Dad left with Andrew for block 54-09…By the way, we called Judy, Andrew's wife, on the radio telephone this afternoon, and she said that our new reservations had been confirmed straight down the line; we would leave on the 14th and arrive in Miami on July 17th…Dad arrived with Andrew last night about 9:00 and said he had shot a rhino and big elephant the day before. The elephant had one 84 pound tusk and one 82 pounder. Pop was now a veteran. I was so glad he had done so well…I wasn't feeling well all the way over here as we rode the last hour in a torrent of rain. I had almost a 100 degree temperature, but as long as I could walk I was diagnosed as OK. The dried riverbeds were bulging with rapid flowing water caused by flash floods in the mountains, and the horses could hardly get across. In camp I read all the next morning and finished the Godfather. Some eland were close by so we left. After walking about 4 miles some natives spooked them, so it was all in vain. Turned back around and came back to camp…Rode and walked until about 6:15 when we finally spotted some impala. The cover was light and they were standing in the open, so I had to take a prone position at a good 300 yards. Squeezed the trigger and knocked it down. I was gratified at making such a long shot, the longest I have ever made. We took pictures as it had a nice rack, and loaded it on a camel. As we headed back to camp it rained again, just long enough to get me all wet…Sambarut and an old man had been ambushed by an elephant that had been waiting for them as they climbed one of our spotting hills to look for game. As they got very near the elephant trumpeted and set out for the old man who started to run. The shot we heard was a warning shot over the elephant's head, and proved to have been enough. The elephant veered and both men made it back to camp."

In a letter to his father dated June 24, 1963, Walter III wrote:

Pop,

We are hunting hard and are still in the process of getting a lion and elephant. Shot an onyx yesterday and 2 other Grant's, that is all. Hope you and Jimmy are having a good hunt.

I figure we should re-connect at least by the 29th so we can change our reservations back home if need be. Andrew says we will meet you on Monday, June 29th, in the evening, at Lodonuhau Base Camp as we can't send a call to Judy about the reservation on Sunday.

Andrew says to tell Judy we are fine and to send her his regards if you happen to hit camp early. Also, if you are there tomorrow, please send some suntan lotion as the sun here is something else. Good hunting and will see you on the 29th as I am looking forward to having a hunting partner.

Love, W.H.B.[3]

Dad and Jimmy's beards are coming along nicely, and I know we are all having a real good time. Nevertheless, a month of hunting is quite a long time, and I think we will all be glad to get back to the States. I must say, you really have to be dedicated to go on one of these foot safaris…Andrew estimated that there were at least 400 elephant in our area, and an equal number in the same area directly next to us. They are coming in because of the rain and the number will possibly increase for the next three weeks. We looked and looked until about 6:15 but could never find the big bull again in the thick brush…Andrew's men forgot to check one of the lion baits yesterday, so when we saw it today, the lion had finished it and had evidently already pushed on…As I looked at the hills for the last time I thought back over the last four weeks, and of all the walking and hunting I have done. It really was quite an experience."

BACK TO LAWYERING

Walter continued to become a leader in various areas of law. One example was when he spoke at a Law-Science Academy trial practice seminar on "Proper Handling of an Aviation Disaster Case," for which he received a certificate of appreciation and recognition exemplifying the infancy of that area of the law at the time. As in other areas of law, Walter was again a true pioneer in aviation law, an area in which he practiced with Aaron Podhurst.

★ ★ ★

When Walter III was in college at Emory, his father had still not encouraged him vocationally. Actually, his father had started inquiring when young Walter was still in junior high as to what his plans were after high school. Young Walter said he thought he might join the Navy as his father had done. Months later, after having carefully considered young Walter's intentions, Walter responded saying he might regret that career choice, and Walter had a proposition to offer him. If he would try college for two years, Walter would pay all costs and expenses, and if he still didn't like school—which young Walter often said he didn't—he could go join the Navy with his father's reluctant blessing. Walter truly believed and silently hoped it would never happen. As time passed, young Walter continued to state his dislike for college. Fortunately, he did stay in college, gaining endearing respect for "the old man's" empathy and intelligence in handling the matter. Surely he must have hoped his son would choose to become an attorney, but recalling Barbara chose another profession, he must have felt strongly *the boy has to make up his own mind and plan for life*. Before obtaining his MBA, Walter III told his father what he was planning to do as a profession, to which Walter simply replied, "Fine, good luck." After graduating and managing money investments for others for two years, young Walter decided to change course and go to law school. When asked why, Walter III said he was very disappointed in the lack of ethics employed by those in the investment business, particularly those in New York City. He believed he might one day be compromised, and disliked the smell of the business. Approaching young Walter about the prospect of law school, his father emphatically said, "If this is about money you're going to be miserable. If it's about service, you're going to be very happy." Young Walter did go to law school and went on to become a very successful lawyer in Atlanta.

Noting young Walter was now seeking advice from his dad, Walter offered more. As a child, Walter was his mother's pride and joy from the day he was born until the day she died. Explaining the difference, Walter said, "Parents aren't supposed to favor one child over another, but all children aren't the same, so some are treated different from their siblings." And so it was that Walter treated each of his children differently from their siblings.

After the elder Walter's mother died, he told young Walter he felt like an orphan, and there may well have been periods when Walter felt very much alone. This feeling may well have caused him to counsel young Walter even further, "the only person in this life that really truly cares about you is you. You come into this world on your own and you will leave it on your own…There will be times you just have to stand up for yourself and fight…There will be times you must be prepared for these days when you will be walking down the street on a fine sunny day, where all could not be more right…when someone steps into your path…hits you in the head with a 2x4 and knocks you down… that is why you must always have a plan." This wise man went even further, cautioning "it is easy just to drift through life when you're young, and just float down the river of life as if on a raft. It will be peaceful and you'll be enjoying yourself…. Then all of a sudden you'll be in your thirties or forties, and many, if not all doors of opportunity will be closed to you. Don't wait that long to have a plan. If you have a wife and kids, you had best start making something of your life. You must have short, medium and long term goals, always moving with a direction and purpose…Yet you must remain flexible, and remember opportunities will most likely knock lightly on your door. You must recognize them. Life is not a dress rehearsal, it is the real thing." What great advice to be given by one whose own life was its best example.

One day in the 1980s, Walter noticed the old wooden baton used by the University of Miami during commencement ceremonies, and decided to donate a replacement in recognition of his long history with the university. It took two and a half years to have a new thirty-pound solid-sterling silver mace crafted so Walter could present it to the then-university president Edward "Tad" Foote. Walter always looked for ways to give back to people or institutions that had helped him grow his legal career.

Author and Walter—
50th Commemorative Ceremony Battle of Midway

As the years past, the Navy saw fit to commemorate the 50th anniversary of the Battle of Midway by holding a memorial gathering at the Navy Museum in Washington, D.C. All survivors of the Battle, and their families and guests, were invited to attend. Walter's family was rather surprised he wanted to go, as he had seldom spoken of those terrible times. Not only was Walter going, but he took his entire family and invited this author and his wife to join them. He wore his service white uniform, and in respect for him, I wore my Marine Corps dress whites uniform. After the ceremony and speeches, Walter was most anxious to see the WWII Memorial, which was recently completed on the Mall. When the entourage stepped out of the fleet of cabs, Walter had some difficulty walking. The crowd of people immediately recognized him as a survivor of that famous battle, and parted the path for him. The respect displayed was somewhat overwhelming for Walter. But it came as no surprise to the rest of us. As a nation and people, we can never sufficiently express our appreciation and gratitude to those who served in that Great War. Kids came up asking for his autograph, and grown men and women stepped forward thanking him for his service. Walter was emotionally moved by all this, but remained stoic and never discussed his feelings about the event when it was over. Did it bring closure for him? Who knows but Walter? What was known is, as always, Walter had a plan to go, do, and see—and he did. For those who were with him, it will always remain in our memories.

A LEGAL LEGEND

Two of Walter's most significant awards came after long service in the field of law. He received the 2004 Hoeveler award, named after the Honorable William M. Hoeveler, senior U.S. district court judge, for personifying both ethics and public service in his fifty-five years as a distinguished lawyer and civic leader. Second, he was recognized as a Legal Legend in 2009, by the 11th Judicial Circuit Historical Society. He was, indeed, a legend in his own time, respected by all in the legal community across the United States.

Renowned Miami attorney, Stuart Grossman, told of being a student in Walter's law and medical class at the University of Miami law school. Being the great teacher Walter was, Stuart recalls vividly how Walter, without using notes, identified and described every bone in the human body starting at the top skull and going all the way down to the metatarsals in the feet. He said, "You need to know all these bones if you are ever to try a case involving injury to any of these." Stuart characterized Walter as being "the epitome of the consummate gentle southern gentleman with a rapier sharp mind…politically astute, a rabid reader who led by example. When a student showed up for class late, claiming how difficult it was to find a parking space in the campus parking lot, Professor Beckham simply said, 'There's plenty of parking at first light.' Walter was one of a kind."

Highly successful and respected attorney Bob Parks knew the name of Walter Beckham long before the two met in 1970, when Bob joined the Podhurst Orseck firm. Bob had the distinct pleasure to work with and try cases with Walter until he, Bob, left the firm in 1988 to open his own law firm. He described Walter as "an extraordinary teacher, lawyer, and intellect who also exuded sound common sense, not often closely associated with the first attributes. He was the most prepared human being in every facet of life. Walter taught me how to try cases the Walter way, always reminding me to never go to court without your trial box, which was usually a standard large file box. Walter's trial box resembled a small stationary store, filled with lined legal pads, pens, pencils, stapler, paper clips, thumb tacks, scotch tape, a hole punch, and anything else one might need to assist in the display of evidence and/or charts, graphs, or other items needing to be made visible to the jury. Walter would be furious if his co-counsel showed up without a fully equipped trial box. It meant you were not prepared for trial. Walter was always prepared for trial. One time I had been trying a case for about six months and asked Walter if he would take a look at the voluminous transcript and offer any comments he thought might assist me in trying the case. Walter took it home over the weekend and returned it on Monday morning, suggesting six or eight elements of the case I had never thought of." Bob closed his remarks saying "no one who has ever received the legal legend award is more deserving than Walter Beckham."

Another very successful Miami lawyer, Ed Moss, met Walter when he, Ed, was a young lawyer in the 1960s. Ed said "Walter made a lasting lifetime impression on this young lawyer. I remember one particular case where I got to observe and participate with Walter. Walter and Perry Nichols displayed their good cop bad cop routine. Perry was the brash, outspoken confrontational lawyer, and Walter was the good cop who tried to patch things up by apologizing for his co-counsel's behavior. It was a treat to watch the two of them try cases in this manner. It wasn't a bad idea, because they almost always won." Ed described Walter as "the consummate polite gentleman who was a student of law and a terrific advocate, who reeked of integrity."

GOING HOME

After receiving the Legal Legend Award, Walter was interviewed by Orlando Rodriguez, a reporter for *The Islander News*. While sitting in his favorite blue robe, sipping lemonade in his Key Biscayne condo, Walter, being forever the consummate teacher, advisor, and counselor, told the reporter, "The law has always been very good to me. I always told my students that every lawyer has the responsibility to put something back into the profession. I chose to do it by teaching."

When asked to recall some of the life he had shared with the law, his eyes glistened as he thought back for a few moments, and then said "I never had the desire to be a judge. That's a hard and restrictive life…One day at Emory, I met an ROTC recruiter who was seeking commissioned officer applicants for the U.S. Naval Reserve." And that was the beginning of his naval career.

Recalling his time aboard the USS *Portland,* during the Battle of Guadalcanal, when his and a flotilla of American ships was being bombarded by the Japanese, he said "Death felt imminent and surviving the fierce battle on that Friday the thirteenth was truly a miracle… One of the great things I love to do is walk on the beach up to the old Cape Florida lighthouse. There's nobody around and you can see hermit crabs crawling around in the sand and the turtles laying their eggs in the sand. As far as traveling goes, I don't need to travel anymore. I've seen everything I needed and wanted to see. Ever since Uncle Sam sent me overseas, I moved throughout the far reaches of the globe. I marveled at the magnitude of Mount Fuji, admired the architecture of the Taj Mahal, hunted big game in Africa with my sons, and saw the beaches of Australia. Key Biscayne has a special place in my heart. I knew it before it was developed." Walter would eventually sell the condo on Key Biscayne, their home in Santa Fe, New Mexico, and leave Miami, resisting Ethel's encouragement for them to move to a new home in Miami, the city where they had spent most of their lives, moving instead to their home in Asheville, North Carolina, in 1999. Walter's active years were over.

The town of Biltmore Forest lies adjacent to the famous Biltmore Estate in Asheville, North Carolina. It is a cluster of luxury homes of historical significance and spacious grounds built in the 1950s. Walter and Ethel loved their home, which was remodeled in 1982 by the renowned architect Henry Gaines. At each side of the entrance to the driveway off the road are two rather large posts with eagles on top. The long uphill driveway of stamped concrete recognizes the seclusion of the house. The grounds are filled with flowering cherry, Bartlet pear, azabar evergreen, magnolia, and weeping cherry trees. Walter's favorite porch swing is on the back porch of the house looking out at the golf course and mountains beyond. Azalea bushes surround the house and a beautiful rose garden is prominent. Inside, one immediately notices the one-and-a-half-story great sitting room with a large fireplace at the far end. A large gold leaf mirror formerly owned by Ethel's grandfather, the once lieutenant governor of Kentucky, hangs above the mantle. A safari room is filled with many of the trophies Walter and his two sons, Walter III and Jimmy, shot when hunting in Kenya. To one side of the room one notices a nice wine cellar of several rows of bottles, each setting inside a length of plumber's PVC pipe crafted by Walter. Upstairs, Walter's bedroom is on the left, painted in royal blue and white with picture frame wall molding. Ethel's bedroom is on the right, decorated in pale peach and turquoise. Both rooms have beautifully carved crown molding, which is also prominent throughout the house. It is easily understandable why Walter chose this home as his last.

He would spend the next two years mostly in his room. He arranged for four hospice caregivers to take care of him, and four for Ethel. And there was the ever faithful and loyal Sabelo Mangena, a big strong man from Zimbabwe who had worked for them as a gardener and all-around handyman for twelve years. Barbara, who lived nearby, was to oversee all their needs and coordinate all the responsibilities of the caregivers. Two hospital beds were brought in, one in each of their rooms, used in place of their own beds. As time went by, Walter and Ethel often remained in their nightclothes, not needing to get dressed. Barbara did not allow visitors, as she wanted all family and friends to remember Walter and Ethel as they used to be, not in the declining physical and mental conditions they were sliding into.

Life was peaceful for them in their old house, far removed from the frantic noisy life of the cities where they had spent most of their lives, where Walter had plied his trade as a lawyer for all those many years. And definitely far removed from the violence and death he had witnessed and experienced in the Pacific so long ago. Walter was going home according to his own plan for doing so. He was in control.

During the late morning hours of October 4, 2011, Dr. Lucian Rice informed Barbara that Walter was dying—a member of the Greatest Generation, a survivor of World War II, and one of the best trial lawyers our nation has ever known. Barbara came quickly, had Sabelo pick up Ethel out of her bed, and bring her into Walter's room. They placed her next to Walter so they could hold hands until Walter expired at 11:10 a.m. They had been married sixty-eight years. His death certificate shows the cause of death to be dementia with lewy bodies, from which he had been suffering for approximately two years.

Services were held at the First United Methodist Church of Coral Gables on October 11. It was a solemn ceremony as one would expect, sprinkled with some remarks that made us smile, and it had its special meaningful moments. Barbara wrote and coordinated the service, which processed with the Navy hymn, and was completed with excerpts from the *Hallelujah Chorus* and *Come Though Almighty King*. Several of Walter's Sunday school notes were read; each extolled Walter's beliefs and how he led his life, which are so relevant in today's world. "Mankind's capacity is the measure of his responsibility... Brotherhood begins at home...Refrain from passing on prejudice to your children...The world cannot afford prejudice. Our future world will either be an age of brotherhood or one of utter destruction...we are determining that future right now." Retired Navy Captain Walter Hull Beckham Jr. was buried in his uniform without military honors, at his request, in a family plot at Woodlawn Park Cemetery North in Miami, Florida. Barbara received the American flag that draped his casket for Ethel, who was too ill to attend. Ethel died December 8, 2012. Walter is survived by his daughter and son-in-law Drs. Barbara DeLeo and James DeLeo, son Walter H. Beckham III, son and daughter-in-law James and Thorne Beckham, five grandchildren, four great-grandchildren, and nine nieces and nephews.

A giant man has passed from among us, but he will never be forgotten.

We salute you, and *Semper Fidelis*, Walter.

EPILOGUE

President Franklin D. Roosevelt died in Warm Springs, Georgia, just twelve days after the Battle of Okinawa (codename Operation Iceberg) began in April 1945. Vice President Harry Truman became president and reviewed the plan to invade mainland Japan (codename Operation Downfall), which had two parts. Operation Olympic was to begin in October of that year, capturing the southern end of Kyushu Island. Operation Coronet was to begin in the spring of 1946, calling for the invasion and capturing of the northern end of Honshu Island, the main island of Japan where Tokyo is located. But the joint chiefs of staff said the plan would only prolong the war, costing upwards of 1 million American casualties and possibly 10 million Japanese lives, because the Japanese would never surrender their homeland—they would die in its defense. Further, the cost to continue to prosecute the war was astronomical in weapons and equipment lost, and it was believed the American people were tired of a war that had cost them so much individually.

Thus, the debate over dropping atomic bombs on Japan created humanitarian and military action concerns. On July 26, 1945, President Truman met with United Kingdom Prime Minister Winston Churchill, and China's Chairman Chiang Kai-shek, issuing the Potsdam Declaration terms for Japan to surrender "or else." It is not clear if the terms of surrender were ever presented to Japan. What is clear is that President Truman chose not to accept the cost involved to continue the war. A mere twelve days later, then-Colonel Paul Tibbets, piloting the "Enola Gay" B-29 with special "Silverplate" modifications, dropped "Little Boy" on Hiroshima, followed three days later by Major Charles Sweeney, piloting "Bocks Car," who dropped "Fat Man" on Nagasaki. Japan surrendered, ending the war in the Pacific. President Truman was faulted by some for dropping the bombs, but he was right. It ended the war and stopped the bloodshed and years more of sacrifice by the people of Japan, the United States, and its allies.

SUMMARY OF

WALTER GOES TO WAR—WWII

When Walter was born in 1920, Japan had invaded Korea and China while the world stood by in disbelief that Japan would ever attack the United States. By the time Walter entered high school, he knew war was imminent with both Japan and Germany. Having already been admitted to Harvard Law School, instead, Walter stepped forward and said, "Take me, I want to serve my country."

In 1854, Japanese Shoguns were learning the ways of Western military forces, and promoting *Hakko Ichiu* (loosely translated to rule the world under one roof). Having failed in the late 1800s, they entered the new century determined to succeed. Read how Pancho Villa served the Japanese and German interests in the early 1900s. The winds of war blew strong. In 1931, Japan invaded Manchuria. While secretly observing the Japanese invasion forces, Marine lieutenant Victor Krulak found the piece of equipment that would later be described as the nexus that enabled us to win World War II.

Walter would serve aboard the USS *Portland* (CA-33) (a heavy cruiser designed to protect battler group aircraft carriers) throughout most of the years he was in the Pacific theater. After six major battles, starting with Midway, Walter would finally stand down. He had been there when Marine sergeant John Basilone earned the Medal of Honor on Guadalcanal; when Marine pilot Major Henderson attacked a Japanese carrier earning a Medal of Honor; and when the *Portland* was torpedoed during the battle for the Solomon Islands.

Read about the first bomber pilot who dropped the first bombs on Berlin, and how members of a tank company from Maywood, Illinois endured and died during the Bataan Death March, only to be subjected to further torture and death in a Japanese prison camp.

Not long after law school, attorney Walter built a career as a legend in the field of law when he and his partner introduced the defense element of law now known as demonstrative evidence. Once the Florida Bar and the courts accepted the practice, and ever since, everyday Americans have reaped financial benefit from their pain and suffering never before seen. Walter was in demand to speak across the country. Many famous defense attorneys attribute their success today as having been students of Walter's in law school. Several landmark cases set Walter apart. He was honest, yet a cunning opponent in court, winning over 95 percent of his cases during a career that lasted more than fifty years.

Read about this giant of a man who passed quietly through life, leaving a mark unequaled by his peers.

ADDENDUM #1

CA33/A16-3/   U. S. S. PORTLAND   11/wfb

June 4, 1942.

From: The Executive Officer.
To :   The Commanding Officer, U.S.S. PORTLAND.

Subject: Battle of Midway - U.S.S. PORTLAND Action -
Report on.

Reference: (a) U.S. Navy Regulations, TP 712.
                 (b) U.S. Navy Regulations, 874(b).
                 (c) PacFlt. ltr. 16CL-42.
                 (d) PacFlt. ltr. 11L-42.
                 (e) OpNav-CominCh joint ltr. #291 dated
February 22, 1942.
                 (f) CinCPac OpOrd serial 2942 dated May 27, 1942.

<u>GENERAL INFORMATION</u>

1.   The PORTLAND, on June 4, 1942, a unit of Task
Force SEVENTEEN, was conducting operations in the general
area north of Midway and in defense of that area, in accordance with reference (f).

Ships present: YORKTOWN (F), ASTORIA, PORTLAND,
MORRIS, HAMMAN, RUSSELL, ANDERSON, HUGHES. The geographical
position at the time of <u>first attack</u> was Latitude 30-42N -
176-48W - and the <u>second attack</u> Latitude 30-42N - 176-40W.
The wind was from the East - force 11 knots - sea, moderate
swell - Sky, blue and 40% clouds alto-cumulus - visibility,
35 miles - barometer, 30.25 - temperature, 71°.

The YORKTOWN had launched her combat and attack
planes at 1030. These squadrons completed attack on enemy
carrier and returned aboard at 1300.

ComTaskFor SEVENTEEN hoisted signal, "One enemy
carrier sunk".

<u>FIRST ATTACK BY THE ENEMY:</u>

2.   At 1401, YORKTOWN signalled a radar contact on a
group of enemy planes bearing 260°T. All ships made ready
to repel attack. This ship was in material condition Zed,
and the crew at General Quarters. Many dog fights were
observed to the West and South, and many planes were shot
down and crashed on fire into the sea. These fights occurred
about 12 miles away, and were a forewarning that the enemy
was ready to start the dive bombing attack. At 1409, the
first enemy dive bomber sighted came out of a cloud and
launched the attack. The action from this point on was fast

Inclosure "E"   - 1 -

ADDENDUM #1 (CONTINUED)

U.S.S. PORTLAND   11/wfb

CA33/A16-3

June 4, 1942.

Subject: Battle of Midway - U.S.S. PORTLAND Action -
                  Report on. (Cont'd).

- -

speed to 17 knots when the enemy launched his torpedo attack.
At least six enemy planes were shot down by our fighters before they arrived at the launching point. Of the five observed
within our zone of fire, three dropped torpedoes close to the
YORKTOWN and two were believed to have hit. One torpedo
passed ahead of the YORKTOWN as the plane was in flames at time
of release. All ships turned to the right away from the attack.
Only one enemy plane of the attack group probably escaped.

From the intense barrage put up by our force it
seems incredible that any plane could pass through and survive.
The YORKTOWN was listing heavily to port and stopped shortly
after the attack. The attack lasted twelve minutes.

At 1657 - YORKTOWN personnel began to "Abandon
ship" - Task Force destroyers recovered the survivors which
were later transferred to the PORTLAND, RUSSELL and MORRIS for
further transfer to the FULTON for return to Pearl Harbor, T.H.

<u>CASUALTIES</u>

4.   The PORTLAND suffered no damage to personnel or
material from the attack. Two barrels of #4 1"1 mount suffered
ruptured muzzles. This same gun suffered one ruptured muzzle
in the Coral Sea action.

<u>COMMENTS</u>

5.   All hands performed their duties in an excellent
manner and no confusion was noted. All hands were eager for
combat and had a definite attitude of self confidence. I
have nothing but praise for the splendid action of our officers
and men in this the "Battle of Midway".

<u>RECOMMENDATION</u>

6.   It is recommended for consideration that a suitable campaign ribbon be authorized to be worn by officers and
men who participated in major naval actions of this type.

                              W. B. COLEMAN,
                        Commander, U.S. Navy.

Enclosure "B"

ADDENDUM #2

10-jrh.

U. S. S. PORTLAND

June 11, 1942.

From: Commanding Officer.
To :   Commander-in-Chief, Pacific Fleet.

Via :   (1) Commander Task Group 17.2.
            (2) Commander Task Force 17.

Subject: Action Report.

References: (a) Arts. 712 and 874(6), U.S. Navy Regs.
            (b) Art. 948, U.S. Navy Regs.

Enclosures: (A) Sketches.
            (B) Report of Executive Officer.

     1.   In compliance with reference (a), the follow-
ing report of action with Japanese aircraft on June 4, 1942,
is submitted herewith:

     (a)   TACTICAL SITUATION

     At 1200, June 4, 1942, the PORTLAND was
operating as a unit of Task Force 17 in accordance with the
organization outlined in Cincpac Operation Plan 29-42. Ships
present were the YORKTOWN, ASTORIA, PORTLAND, MORRIS, ANDERSON,
HAMMANN, RUSSELL and HUGHES. The Task Force was in Disposition
"V", on axis 225 T., fleet course was 225 T., and fleet speed
was 25 knots. Circle spacing was 1000 yards. PORTLAND was on
station 2300. O.T.C. (Commander Task Force 17), and guide were
in the YORKTOWN at the center. The geographical position was
Latitude 30-39-00 N., Longitude 176-39-00 W. The wind was from
S.S.E., 9 knots; sky was clear with about 30 percent alto-
stiatus; sea was slight with moderate swell from S.S.E. Ship
was keeping plus 10 zone time.

     (b)   PRELIMINARY ACTION

     An enemy force had been sighted by patrol planes
about 150 miles to the northwest of Midway. Task Force 17 was
operating in an area bearing 15 T., 175 miles from Midway. The
YORKTOWN had launched an attack group at about 1030. Prior to
the return of this group the YORKTOWN made two radar contacts
on strange aircraft - one at 1258, bearing 310 T., distant 25
miles and one at 1310, bearing 262 T., distant 39 miles. At
1333 the Task Force changed course to 070 T. while the YORKTOWN
was engaged in recovering the attack group previously mentioned.

ADDENDUM #2 (CONTINUED)

CA33/A16-3
Serial 043.

10-jrh.

U. S. S. PORTLAND

June 11, 1942.

Subject: Action Report.

(b)(Continued)

During the period of recovery two more radar contacts were made by the YORKTOWN, one at 1352 on a group of strange aircraft bearing 265 T., distant 30 miles and one at 1401 on a group of strange aircraft bearing 260 T., distant 15 miles. At 1403 sighted enemy plane.

(c)   CHRONOLOGICAL ORDER OF EVENTS

1200 - On station 2300 in Disposition "V", axis 225 T.; base course 225 T.&G., fleet speed 25 knots. Ship was in Condition of Readiness III with the A.A. Battery in Condition I; Material Condition "Z" with few scuttles open for ventilation.

1204 - Commenced zig-zag plan 41 on base course 240 T.

1219 - Ceased zig-zagging and steadied on course 290 T.

1226 - Commenced zig-zag plan 41 on base course 290 T.

1248 - Ceased zig-zagging and steadied on course 135 T.

1258 - YORKTOWN made radar contact on strange aircraft bearing 318 T., distant 25 miles.

1301 - Changed fleet course to 290 T.

1310 - YORKTOWN made radar contact on strange aircraft bearing 262 T., distant 39 miles.

1333 - Changed course to 070 T. following movements of YORKTOWN during aircraft operations.

1352 - YORKTOWN made radar contact on a group of strange aircraft bearing 265 T., distant 30 miles.

1401 - YORKTOWN made radar contact on a group of strange aircraft bearing 260 T., distant 15 miles.

1403 - Sighted enemy plane in dog fight with own fighter on bearing 060 T.

ADDENDUM #2 (CONTINUED)

```
CA33/A16-3                              10-jrh.
Serial 043.
                  U. S. S. PORTLAND

                                   June 11, 1942.

Subject:      Action Report.
- - - - - - - - - - - - - - - - - - - - - - - -

        (c)(Continued)

        1404 - General Quarters - set Material Condition
"Z" throughout the ship.

        1405 - Began maneuvering on various courses at
various speeds following movements of YORKTOWN.

        1409 - Several enemy planes approached the
formation to deliver dive bombing attack.  Commenced firing.
Position:  Latitude 30-42-00 N., Longitude 176-48-00 W.  Wind
was from S.E., force 11 knots.  Sky was clear with forty per-
cent alto-cumulus clouds.  Sea was calm with moderate swell
from S.E.

        1413 - Observed near miss astern of YORKTOWN.

        1414 - Observed direct bomb hit on YORKTOWN
flight deck in the vicinity of the stack.  YORKTOWN began
smoking heavily.

        1415 - Attack completed.  Ceased firing.  Began
maneuvering on various courses at 20 knots to screen the
YORKTOWN while that ship extinguished fires incident to bomb
hits.

        1451 - Sighted four ships bearing 112 T. and
identified them as friendly.

        1520 - VINCENNES, PENSACOLA, BENHAM and BALCH
joined the group screening the YORKTOWN.

        1602 - YORKTOWN underway at 5 knots on course
090 T.

        1610 - Received signal from O.T.C. to be pre-
pared to repel aircraft attack.

        1619 - On signal from O.T.C. took station
2225 in disposition "V", circle spacing 1000 yards, course
and axis 090 T., speed 10 knots, YORKTOWN at center, guide.

        1620 - Changed fleet speed to 12 knots.

        1623 - Changed fleet speed to 15 knots.
```

ADDENDUM #2 (CONTINUED)

CA33/A16-3
Serial 043.

U. S. S. PORTLAND

10-jrh.

June 11, 1942.

Subject: Action Report.
- -

(c)(Continued)

1626 - Changed fleet speed to 17 knots.

1630 - Changed fleet speed to 15 knots.

1633 - O.T.C. executed signal to all ships less YORKTOWN to zig-zag independently.

1635 - Received signal from O.T.C. to prepare to repel aircraft attack.

1637 - YORKTOWN increased speed to 19 knots.

1639 - Sighted enemy plane shot down by YORKTOWN fighter on the port beam. O.T.C. executed signal for all ships less YORKTOWN steam at 25 knots.

1640 - Enemy torpedo planes began attack. Attack was concentrated on the YORKTOWN. Position: Latitude 30-42-00 N., Longitude 176-40-00 W. Wind was from E., force 14 knots. Sky was blue with about forty percent alto-cumulus clouds. Sea was calm with moderate swells from S.E. Commenced firing with all weapons. Began maneuvering radically to maintain station on the YORKTOWN and to evade torpedoes.

1642 - It was apparent that YORKTOWN had been hit by a torpedo on the port side. YORKTOWN began circling to the left.

1650 - It was noted that the YORKTOWN had developed a heavy list to port.

1652 - Enemy withdrew. Ceased firing. YORKTOWN stopped. Cruisers and Destroyers began radical zig-zag circling the YORKTOWN at 25 knots.

1657 - YORKTOWN began abandoning ship.

1705 - Received signal from O.T.C. to be prepared to repel aircraft attack.

1711 - Received signal from O.T.C. that radar contact had been made and enemy aircraft sighted on bearing 135 T. Sighted and identified ships of Task Force 16 bearing 111 T.

-4-

ADDENDUM #2 (CONTINUED)

.33/A16-3
Serial 043.   10-jrn.

U. S. S. PORTLAND

June 11, 1942.

Subject: Action Report.

- -

(c)(Continued)

1715 - Observed dog fight between enemy plane and friendly fighter. Destroyers began rescue of YORKTOWN personnel.

1910 - Cruisers formed column on ASTORIA (guide) with destroyers forming Inner Anti-submarine Screen. Course 090 T., speed 15 knots.

(d)   THE ATTACKS

The subject engagement divided itself into two separate and distinct phases.

(a) Phase I.

At 1352 Z.T. (plus 10) with Task Force Seventeen in formation "Victor", base course and force axis 225 T., on recovery course 070°, speed 25 knots, the YORKTOWN made radar contact with enemy planes, bearing 265 T., distance 30 miles. The A.A. Battery was in Condition I. At 1401 a second contact was made bearing 260 T., distance 15 miles. At 1403 a series of four large splashes accompanied by smoke was observed on the horizon, bearing 250 T. Almost immediately thereafter, many individual dog fights were observed with subsequent plane crashes, plane burnings and parachute descensions. This action took place over a wide sector, from about 090 T. to about 270 T. Few, if any, enemy planes appeared to be in the clear until almost overhead in position for their dive attack. Anti-aircraft fire was deliberately delayed because enemy planes were being engaged by our own fighters.

At 1409 two dive bombers appeared overhead apparently having come in on bearing 160 T., and four emerged from the melee bearing 270 T. These planes were engaged by both automatic weapons and anti-aircraft guns. One bomber made a near miss on the carrier and dove into the sea having been hit by gunfire. A second bomber was seen to crash into the sea after bomb release. A third bomber was seen to make a wide miss on the carrier and likewise crashed. A fourth plane was disintegrated in the air, probably by a burst from the PORTLAND'S 5"/25 cal. battery, which was laying down a director controlled barrage on the port quarter. Another plane was seen to dive on the YORKTOWN and release its bomb after having been hit. The bomb from this latter plane hit the carrier in the vicinity of the stack and the plane crashed into the sea off the port bow of the carrier.

-5-

ADDENDUM #2 (CONTINUED)

CA33/A16-3   10-jrh.
Serial 043.
                        U. S. S. PORTLAND

                              June 11, 1942.

Subject: Action Report.
- -

        (d)(a)(Continued)

            It is estimated that eighteen Japanese dive
bombers approached the formation. Twelve of these were brought
down by our defensive fighters. Six penetrated the anti-aircraft
screen. One of these six was disintegrated before bomb release.
The remaining five planes made their dive bombing attack,
released their bombs and crashed. Not one enemy plane was seen
effecting a successful retirement from the engagement.
            At 1415 the attack was completed; "cease firing"
was ordered. The YORKTOWN was smoking heavily and was being
screened by the other vessels of the Task Force. At 1520 the
VINCENNES, PENSACOLA, BENHAM and BALCH joined the formation.

        (b) Phase II.
            At 1610 the signal to prepare to repel aircraft
attack was received. At 1619 the augmented task force assumed
formation "Victor", circle spacing 1000 yards, base course and axis
090 T., speed 10 knots. At 1630 speed was increased to 15 knots
and at 1635 the 1610 signal was repeated.
            At 1636 a loose formation of planes was picked
up bearing 080 T., distance 9 miles. Altitude was 7000 feet.
A solution (5"/25 cal. port battery) was obtained but fire was
not opened immediately because of recognition difficulties. At
1639 one of these planes was dived on by a plane recognized as
a friendly fighter. One torpedo plane fell in flames. Fire
was then opened using straight director solution. Bursts
appeared close, were spotted on; one plane fell. When the
problem had run to 3000 yards a barrage was started and at the
same time all automatic weapons that would bear, opened fire.
Other vessels of the force layed down barrages in the path of
the oncoming Japanese torpedo planes in an effort to prevent
them from reaching their objective, the carrier. The result-
ant fire appeared to cover the attacking planes from all angles,
the volume was amazing. The main battery fired a barrage into
the water but the five rounds expended fell "over" instead of
"short" of the last planes to come in. It seemed incredible that
any attacking planes could penetrate this heavy barrage successfully. It is believed that four torpedo planes were successful
in releasing their torpedoes well inside of 500 yards, three of
which hit the carrier. Two of these were hit prior to release
but did not crash until they had reached the unengaged side.
Two are believed to have safely retired from the action.
            The YORKTOWN listed heavily to port as the attack
ended at 1652. She stopped completely and at 1657 she was
abandoned.

                        -6-

ADDENDUM #2 (CONTINUED)

CA33/A16-3
Serial 043.

10-jrh.

U. S. S. PORTLAND

June 11, 1942.

Subject: Action Report.

- -

(d)(b)(Continued)

At 1705 a signal was received to prepare to repel an aircraft attack. This attack did not materialize. Ammunition expenditure was as follows:

BATTERY	ROUNDS FIRED	PERCENT OF ALLOWANCE
8"/55 Cal.	5	0.4
5"/25 Cal.	235	9.
1.10/75 Cal.	1440	4.
20 mm.	3200	9.

(e)   CASUALTIES

Premature bursts occurred in barrels #1 and #4 of 1.10, Mount IV. Barrel #1 ruptured eight inches from the muzzle and both the muzzle and the water jacket were blown off. The muzzle and part of the water jacket of barrel #4 were blown off when the former ruptured approximately five inches from the muzzle. The mount was put out of commission temporarily while the water leads were plugged after which time barrels #2 and #3 were serviceable.

This was the second and third time respectively that this casualty has occurred on this mount in the past month. It is attributable to faulty ammunition, (Index - SPD 2828).

There were no personnel casualties.

(f)   COMMENTS AND OBSERVATIONS

(1)   GUNNERY
(a)
It is interesting to note that the dive bombing and torpedo plane attacks were not coordinated. Each attack was separate and distinct, a lull of some two and a half hours existing between the two.

The dive bombing attack was well broken up by our defending fighters as the bombers attempted penetration of the screen. A melee accordingly developed in which anti-aircraft battery defense was of necessity subordinated to defense by own fighters. The bombers were in this manner well dispersed. Approximately twelve enemy dive bombers were downed by fighters. Six planes penetrating the screen were widely scattered

-7-

ADDENDUM #2 (CONTINUED)

CA33/A16-3
Serial 043.   10-jrh.

U.S.S. PORTLAND

June 11, 1942.

Subject: Action Report.

- -

(f)(1)(a)(Continued)

dove from several different bearings in confusion. Two such
bombers nearly collided while delivering their attacks. The
attacking torpedo planes of the second phase faired better and
were not so completely routed for, although only six or seven
of these penetrated the screen, they kept together during the
final stages of the attack.

(b)
The 5"/25 Cal. battery was employed to much
better advantage in defense of the carrier during this engagement than during that of the Coral Sea. A well executed
barrage was controlled by the director during each phase of
the engagement and the fact that one plane was brought down
in each phase proved gratifying. It is felt that this barrage
would have proved even more successful had the attacking planes
not been so widely dispersed prior to diving and had followed
in each other's wake at regular intervals as has been customary
in the past.

During the first phase the port 5"/25 Cal.
director was trained in the direction of the YORKTOWN and was
elevated to about 40°. The rangekeeper was set up with target
speed (0), own ship's speed (0), own ship's course set
continuously, stable element running and cut in. Range and
position angle were cranked into values taken from precomputed
tabular values based on our distance from the YORKTOWN at the
time. Thus the director was set to place a barrage between
carrier and attacking planes at an instant's notice. Actually
the first dive bomber did not approach in our sector (assumed to
be that sector toward and beyond carrier) and so a snap range
was obtained and fire opened immediately. The barrage was well
placed and the volume of fire, high. The third plane to attack
near this bearing was disintegrated by a 5"/25 Cal. burst,
believed to have been from this barrage.

In the second phase, torpedo planes were sighted
early enough to obtain a director solution and the port battery
opened fire at a range of about 8000 yards. The attacking
torpedo planes were followed in, and at a range of about 3000
yards after they had broken up and formed an approximate column,
the director time motor was stopped and director pointer and
trainer matched "generated", and a barrage instituted immedi-
this barrage was also well placed in the path of the oncom-

ADDENDUM #2 (CONTINUED)

CA33/A16-3
Serial 043.

10-jrh.

U. S. S. PORTLAND

June 11, 1942.

Subject: Action Report.

- -

(f)(1)(b)(Continued)

       This planned employment of the 5"/25 Cal. battery appears to have been far more effective than the rather wild local control fire of the same battery in the Coral Sea. Some such employment of the batteries of the Task Force might increase the protection of what has so far been the enemy's sole objective - the carrier.

(c)

       Improvement was observed in fire control of automatic weapons since the Coral Sea engagement. Emphasis has been placed on defense of vessel being screened and the necessary instruction in sufficient lead-off has produced results. Tracer control is now used against all targets presenting deflection rates while straight ring sight control is retained for use against "no deflection" targets attacking this vessel direct. Considerable sleeve firing during recent weeks has contributed a measure of much needed and valued experience.

(d)

       Nearly all the planes in both phases approached the outer limits of effective range which was just within the tracer burn out point. The fire on these was well controlled and there was no wild shooting. No friendly planes were inadvertently fired on.

(e)

       Ammunition supply was adequate; replacement closely followed expenditure. The present allowance of 15-20 mm magazines should prove sufficient for all actions.

(f)

       No mechanical difficulties or stoppages were experienced with any automatic weapon.

(2)   <u>SHIP CONTROL</u>

       The ship was conned by the Captain and Navigator on the bridge. In the Coral Sea the ship was conned from the catwalk outside the conning tower. It is believed that in an air attack, where the ship is making frequent and large changes of course it is better to control from the bridge where communication with the bridge personnel is close rather than through conning tower slits or conning tower door. In addition the Captain has better visibility and can keep

ADDENDUM #2 (CONTINUED)

10-jrh.

U. S. S. PORTLAND

June 11, 1942.

Subject: Action Report.

(2)(Continued)

closer contact with the developing situation.

(3) GENERAL

The conduct of the officers and crew was in accordance with the best traditions of the Service. All were calm throughout the action and the fire discipline was excellent.
All hands performed their duties well and no one officer or man can be singled out for special commendation.

2.   The report of the Executive Officer, required by reference (b), is forwarded herewith as Enclosure (B), in compliance with reference (a).

L.T. DUBOSE.

Original: Cincpac (1 copy).
Copy to : CTG 17.2,
          CTF 17,
          War Diary.

ADDENDUM #2 (CONTINUED)

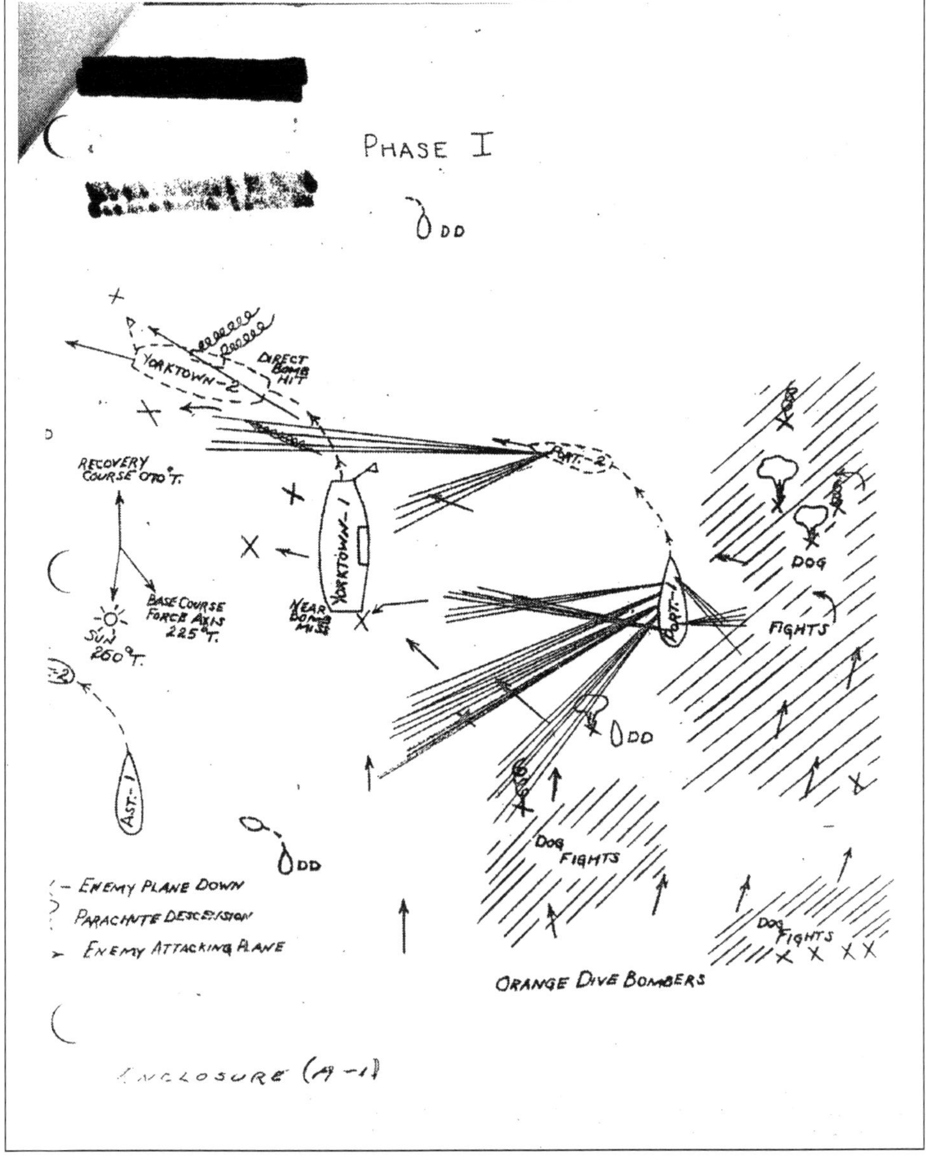

ADDENDUM #2 (CONTINUED)

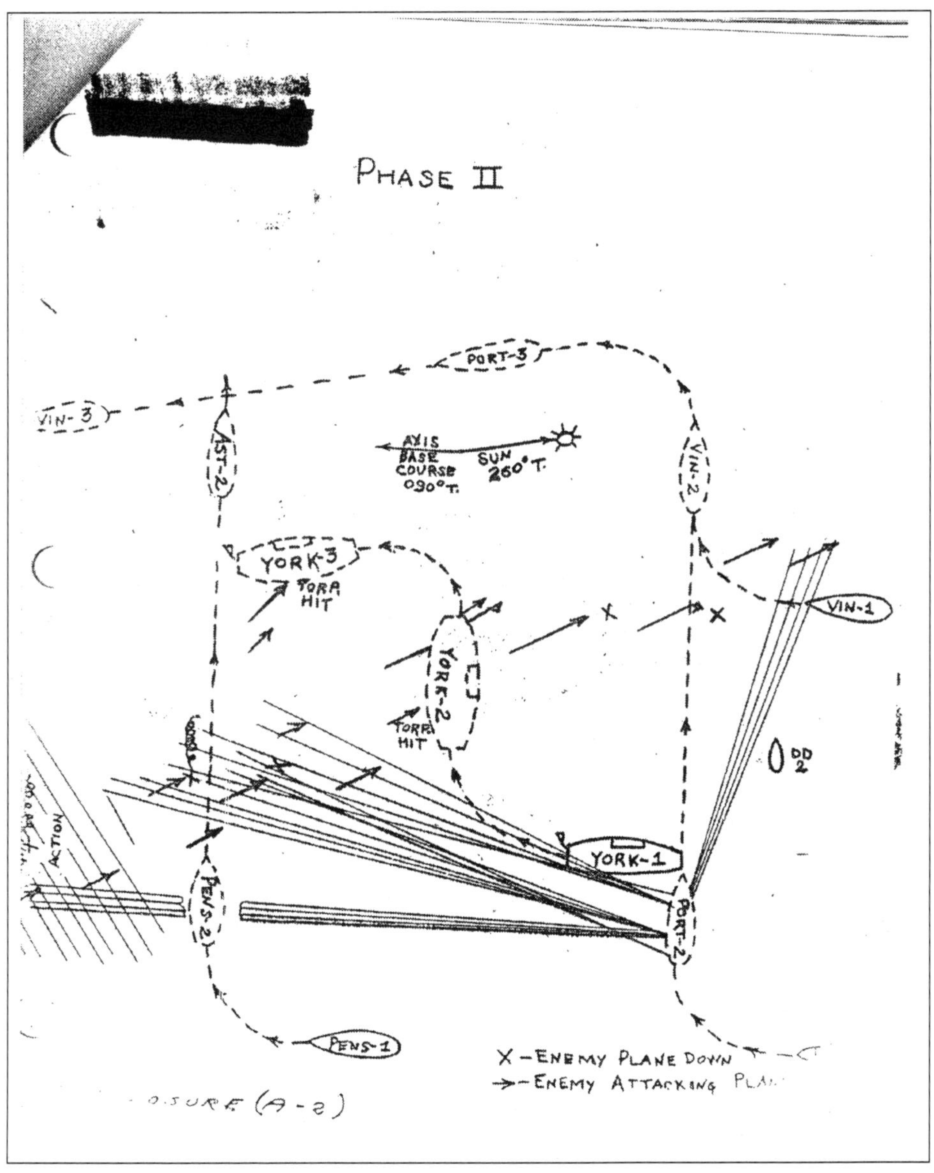

ABOUT THE AUTHOR

DICK HREBIK

DICK HREBIK is an author, historian, adjunct lecturer, actor, singer, adventurer, and retired Marine mustang major who brings humor and challenging questions to his books and speeches. He holds an MBA degree and is an arbitrator for the Financial Industry National Regulatory Authority (FINRA). For twenty-two years he was the Director of Administration of large law firms, including the Washington, DC office of Jones Day. He is a voice from the Silent Generation who has traveled to and/or lived in ninety-six countries, having climbed some of the highest mountains in the world.

BOOKS:

So, You Want a Job?

Corps Vet

The Warrior Among Us
(winner of 2011 National Stars and Flags Book Award & the prestigious 2012 Military Writers Society of America Book Award for political science fiction)

SPEECHES:

Secrets and Spies

What's Wrong in America

27809519R00099

Made in the USA
Lexington, KY
24 November 2013